insects from close up

insects from close up

Photographs by HARRY F. BREVOORT

Text by ELEANOR IVANYE FANNING

THOMAS Y. CROWELL COMPANY

New York / Established 1834

contents

illustrations

insects from close up

six legs

Insects are a nuisance. They bother us. Some bite. Some sting. Some carry diseases. Others ruin picnics, invade kitchens, or infest closets. Still others destroy crops, spoil fruit, or kill trees; each year insects do twice the damage to forests that fires do.

Yet this would be a poor world without them. All insects are fascinating. Some are beautiful; some ugly. Insects are food for birds and bats, for fish and frogs, and even for other insects. Many are scavengers, returning to the soil minerals that are vital for new life. Insects give us wax, honey, silk, and shellac. But their greatest gift is to help plants grow. As they search for food, many insects cross-fertilize plants, carrying pollen from one flower to another, thereby increasing fruit and seed production. Bees are well known for these services, but other insects—butterflies and moths, flies, wasps and beetles—help, too.

How Many Insects? Both in number and variety, insects are overwhelming. There are so many kinds that if you learned the names of one hundred insects every day, it would take you over twenty years to learn all the known insects. Scientists have described about 800,000 species of insects throughout the world, but they estimate that there may be ten times as many still unnamed, most of them to be found in the tropics.

Incredible as it may seem, there are more than twice as many kinds of insects as the total number of kinds of all other living things—both plants and animals. And at any given time, the total number of individual insects of all species is astronomical.

Insects are found over almost all the earth. They can live in deserts, hot springs, snow fields and caves, in quiet ponds and swift rivers, in forests, meadows, and swamps. Only salt water seems to give insects pause; there are few ocean-going insects.

Is It an Insect? Not every tiny creature that crawls or hops is an insect. If you're in doubt, count its legs. If there are six, it is an insect. If there are more or less than six, it's not.

The body of an insect is divided into three sections, each with standard

1

Two enormous compound eyes (each about the size of a pea) enable the dragonfly to see in almost every direction. One eye may have as many as 30,000 hexagonal lenses.

attachments. First comes the head with antennae, eyes, and mouthparts. The antennae, or "feelers," are used for hearing, tasting, and smelling. They vary greatly in shape and size. Many insects have two different kinds of eyes. There are tiny, simple eyes with one lens each, which only distinguish light from dark. And there are larger, compound eyes, sometimes composed of thousands of individual hexagonal lenses, which are used to detect motion. Neither kind of eye can be focused, however. Most insects are nearsighted.

There are two kinds of insect mouthparts, each composed of many complex parts. Some insects have mouthparts adapted for chewing or biting, others for piercing and sucking.

Insects have no necks. The head is directly attached to a middle section called the thorax, which is the center of motion. All six legs and the wings, if they are present, are attached here.

All insects have six legs. The walking stick, below, is protected by color and shape, which blend with the leaves and twigs of the trees it inhabits. Contrary to its name, this insect walks awkwardly. It is frequently motionless by day, but chews on leaves at night.

The main functions of the tapering abdomen behind the legs and thorax are digestion and reproduction. On this last section of the insect, females have an organ especially suited for laying eggs—the ovipositor. In some insects, this is connected to venom glands and has been modified to be used as a stinger.

An Exterior Skeleton Instead of having bones inside the skin, the body of an insect has its rigid, supporting tissue outside. This exterior skeleton, or exoskeleton, is made of chitin (*kye*-tin), a waterproof layer that is resistant to most chemicals, and covers the entire body. Although it is thinner and more flexible at the joints, this armor cannot expand with growth. Periodically, the insect must shed the old suit. It splits, usually down the back. Then the insect crawls out and rapidly expands before the new armor—already formed under the old—can harden in the air.

The muscles that move the legs and wings are attached directly to the exoskeleton. This is a very efficient arrangement, but it means that with each shedding muscles must be attached to the new skeleton forming underneath. An insect is always motionless for a day or two before molting because it needs the time for reattachment.

Working muscles need air. However insect respiration is very different from human respiration. Insects have no lungs. Instead, air diffuses directly into tiny oval openings, called spiracles, that lie along the sides of the insect's body. On large insects, the spiracles are easy to see, especially along the abdomen. Some insects—particularly pond dwellers—can open and close their spiracles, a trick they use when diving.

Each spiracle, in turn, leads into an air tube, or trachea, which has spirally braced walls to prevent collapse. The trachea divides and redivides into very fine tubes which lead air to all parts of the body. In some insects the tracheae end in air sacs, which both store air and increase buoyancy.

In human beings oxygen is carried from the lungs to all parts of the body by the red pigment, or hemoglobin, in our blood. Insects have no such oxygen-carrying red pigment although a few insects may have red blood. Usually insect blood is straw-colored and clear. Nor does it circulate as human blood does in a closed system of arteries and veins. When the insect's heart contracts, blood is simply pumped out. It oozes through the body spaces and eventually returns to the heart again.

These simple systems of breathing and blood circulation are fine for very small animals, but are much too inefficient for big ones. This is why any insect longer than an inch is a large insect.

Insects are cold-blooded animals, lacking the mammal's means of maintaining a constant body temperature. Man has a built-in thermostat that allows body chemical processes to go on at the same rate all year round. Our

The hard, shiny shell of the grasshopper is really the skeleton which holds its body together. Like other insects, it has no bones or internal support. Thinner, flexible areas around the joints enable the insect to move.

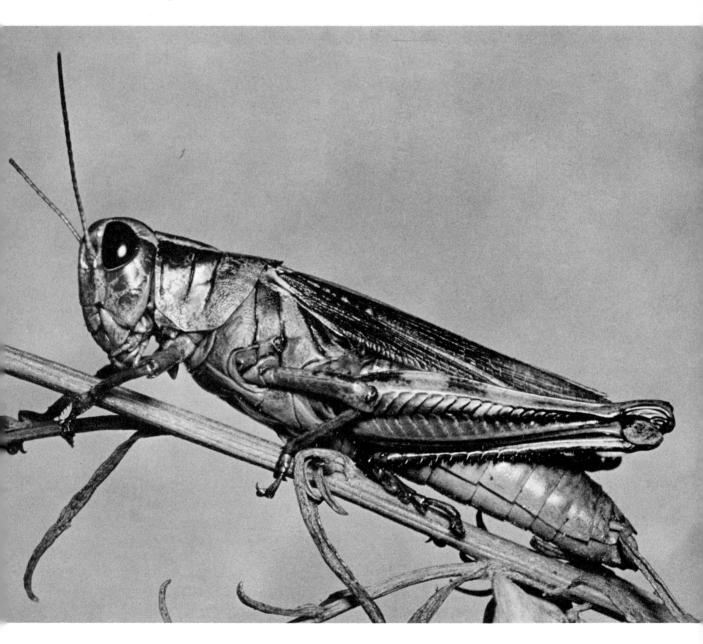

The outgrown skin splits down the back, allowing the insect to escape. The new skeleton then hardens in the air. Here, the empty shell of a dragonfly clings to a plant stem a few inches above the water. The entire body of the adult burst through the small opening at the thorax.

This close-up of a grasshopper's head shows the texture of its shell. Because this hard covering does not stretch, the insect will shed the skin when it becomes too small.

muscles contract just as quickly in winter as in summer. But an insect has no such control. Its body is the same temperature as the surrounding air or water. When it is hot, chemical processes go on at a faster rate. An insect can move quickly. But as air temperature drops, chemical processes slow down. Insect muscles do not function so rapidly. The insect becomes more and more sluggish. Insects cannot fly when the air temperature is below 50 degrees F. and insects that live in the north must hibernate in protected places in order to survive the winter months.

Two Ways of Growing Up   All insects begin as eggs. Where and when the eggs are laid depends on the kind of insect. Grasshoppers lay eggs in the ground in fall; dragonflies drop their eggs into ponds in summer; butterflies deposit their eggs on leaves in spring.

When they hatch, some insects look like their parents except that they are smaller and lack wings. Then, each time the exoskeleton is shed, the young nymph increases one step in size, and sprouts larger and larger wing pads. After half a dozen molts, the wings reach full size, and the insect is an adult, able to reproduce. For the rest of its life—which may be a few hours or more than a year—the insect will not grow or shed its skin again. Grasshoppers and

Insects are easy to catch, if not to photograph. Equipped with jars and nets, two boys search a meadow for insects. Nets are available at hobby and department stores. Or an effective net can be made at home from a broomstick, a coat hanger, and cheesecloth.

Many insects get away between jar and net. But fewer escape if this procedure is followed: Place the mouth of the jar over the insect while it is still inside the net.

dragonflies follow this three-stage pattern of egg, nymph, and adult in growing up.

Other insects look very different from their parents when they hatch—so different that some kind of magic seems to be involved. The egg hatches into a larva that looks like a worm, moves slowly, and has no external sign of wings. It concentrates on eating, growing, and storing up energy. It molts several times to accommodate its increasing bulk. Finally it stops eating and is very quiet for a day or two. The larval skin then splits for the last time, revealing a new stage, the pupa. Now it looks dead and shapeless. But inside the pupa, the body of the larva is being rebuilt into the body of the adult. When the process is complete, the adult emerges from the pupa case, fully mature, able to fly and reproduce. It will grow no more, but concentrates on finding a mate and laying eggs. Butterflies and moths, flies, beetles, and ants follow this strange four-stage life pattern. The four-stage life pattern is termed complete metamorphosis, meaning "complete change," because the immature insect is entirely different from the adult. The three-stage life pattern is called incomplete metamorphosis, meaning "incomplete change," because the nymph is merely an immature form of the adult—its parts will mature and grow, but they will never undergo a complete change.

In order to simplify learning about insects, scientists have divided them into about twenty groups, called orders. These are based on patterns of growth and the design and function of legs, wings, and mouthparts. This system of classification makes it easy to recognize insects that are closely related and it is the one followed in the following chapters.

the straight wings

Three hundred million years ago enormous cockroaches prowled the hot and humid swamps that covered the continents. It was a silent world, relatively safe for the few kinds of insects that hunted in the lush vegetation, for there were as yet no birds and no mammals. Man himself did not appear until a mere million years ago.

Only in size are modern roaches different from their ancient relatives. Fossils found in coal show that roaches once grew to be four inches long; now a cockroach that is an inch long is a giant. But their flattened bodies are the same. They have always found it easy to hide in crevices. They still have two pairs of wings, too. The front pair, thickened and leathery, lies straight back on their bodies. The thinner hind wings lie underneath, folded like a fan. Their chewing mouthparts, with jaws that move from side to side, make it possible for roaches to eat any kind of food, plant or animal. If discovered, they can make a fast getaway because their equal-sized legs make them good runners.

Some species of roaches make a good living scavenging in the woods, while others have adapted to man's habits, traveling everywhere with him, staying active all year in heated buildings, finding abundant food as they hunt in the dark.

Family characteristics make cockroach cousins (order Orthoptera— straight winged) easy to recognize. Straight wings and chewing jaws are also typical of grasshoppers and crickets, praying mantises and walking sticks. But only the crickets are still omnivorous. The other groups specialize. All follow the three-stage growth pattern. Winter is spent in the egg. In spring the nymphs hatch, looking like miniature, wingless adults. Most of the summer is spent in growing. Usually we notice the adults only in late summer. They lay eggs then and, having insured a perpetuation of the species, die soon after fall's first frosts.

Walking Sticks   The narrow, knobby, three-inch-long bodies of walking sticks beautifully camouflage them, making them seem like brown or green twigs on trees. Their long slender legs and elongate antennae add to the deception, but at the expense of maneuverability. Walking sticks walk very awkwardly. By day they may not even move at all, but instead assume cataleptic poses on oaks and wild cherry trees, for these insects are primarily nocturnal. During the night they are busy consuming leaves. If many walking sticks inhabit a tree, a disastrous number of leaves may disappear in short order.

After two summer months of munching and molting, walking sticks are full-sized, but the northern species hardly ever grow wings. (They are extra baggage in any case, for another leaf is just a lurch away.) In late summer, each female lays as many as a hundred eggs, dropping them one by one to the forest floor, where they remain all winter. If walking sticks are numerous, it can actually seem to rain eggs. These eggs look just like seeds: hard, shiny and black, with a white stripe around the edge. Compared to most insect eggs, they are huge, measuring an eighth of an inch long.

In contrast to the enormous cockroaches of prehistoric times, this German cockroach nymph perches easily on the end of a clothespin. Full grown, it is about an inch long.

The Praying Mantis The praying mantis could easily win a prize for size, growing to a length of three and a half inches. It wins hands down (or claws up) for voracious appetite. Neither a runner nor a jumper, it simply stalks or waits in the green shrubbery it matches so well until something edible walks by. A quick lunge with its murderously spined grasping claws impales the victim. A quick bite—usually in the tender skin just behind the head—and the captive struggles no more. Bite by bite, the soft body is consumed, the inedible wings and legs dropping to the ground. Then the mantis may turn its triangular head for a glance over its shoulder—another feat most insects cannot equal—to see what morsel it might have missed during the snack. Or it may simply settle down again to wait for another meal to wander by, keeping its front claws upraised in pious pose. But the chances are that the mantis will begin the delicate job of cleaning its antennae and eyes, legs and face, grooming thoroughly and carefully before hunger strikes again.

From the time it hatches in early June as a mosquito-sized, tan, wingless replica of the adult, the mantis is hungry. Its first meals are aphids, but they may also be a brother or sister mantis if one happens to be near. Somehow, the female seems to know this when she is building the dun-colored, walnut-sized egg case in the fall, for she constructs a separate tiny room for each of the 350 eggs she lays. The egg case is foamy while it is being built, but gradually hardens during winter and spring. When the mantis hatches, it dangles briefly from the egg case by a thread, but soon leaves to begin eating. Its appetite and capacity increase from aphid- to grasshopper-sized meals by late August, when the mantis is mature and has full-sized wings. Mating takes place then, and often after this the female turns cannibal and eats the male. Then, clinging head down to a twig, she constructs the egg case, never once looking backward. Organs at the end of her abdomen build the complex structure automatically in about three hours.

Because they eat so many insects, mantises are immeasurably beneficial in gardens. Some are even kept as pets. (There is no penalty for confining any insect in the United States.) If a mantis is kept as a pet in fall, there is no harm done, for its days of voracious eating are almost over, and, as the machinery runs down, the mantis simply dies.

The "Short Horns" Armed only with sideways-moving jaws, grasshoppers and locusts can, and do, cause fearful devastation to crops all over the world. They have been a plague, particularly in arid regions, and have caused famines because their appetites, en masse, can literally sweep a field clean of everything green.

Antennae shorter than their bodies have earned these insects the nickname "short horns." Like the roaches, their front wings are straight and leathery and their hind wings pleated like a fan, sometimes brightly colored. Some grasshoppers rattle their wings in flight.

Long, spiny legs make cockroaches good runners. And after the getaway, their sleek bodies fit in narrow crevices where bulkier enemies cannot get to them.

Few insects escape the firm grasp of the praying mantis, shown here devouring a two-course meal. While eating the first course in its left claw, it holds the rest of its meal in the right. A giant among insects, the mantis grows to a length of three and a half inches.

At first glance it looks more like a snake than an insect, but this triangular head actually belongs to a praying mantis. Huge compound eyes bulge out from two corners. Three simple eyes form another triangle between the bases of the antennae.

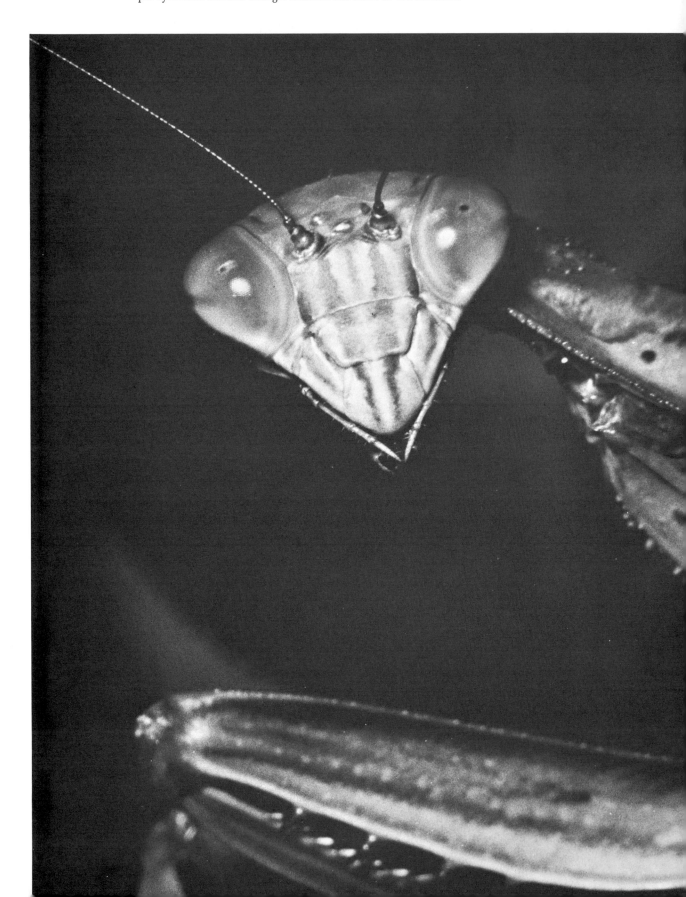

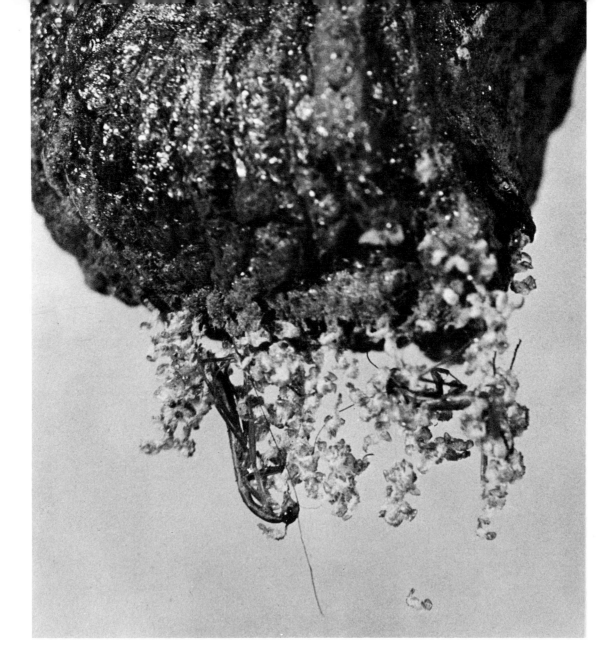

Newly hatched from the egg case, a mosquito-sized mantis dangles by a thread until its soft skin hardens in the air. The case contains separate rooms for each of the 350 eggs laid by its mother. Such privacy protects the unhatched egg from its hungry brothers and sisters.

Grasshoppers' enormously developed hind legs give them their jumping power. One push with the strong muscles that work these legs, and the mature insect may leap twenty times its body length. Some sand-colored grasshoppers seem to disappear the moment they land, so well do they blend with their background.

The male grasshopper has strong spines on his hind legs, which he uses as a primitive musical instrument, much as children use the teeth of a comb. He rasps these spines against the thickened edges of his front wings. With this music he lures a mate, for even though the female can't make music, she can hear. There are tiny oval "eardrums" on the sides of the abdomen in both males and females.

Once the female has mated, she digs a short burrow in the ground with the ovipositor at the end of her abdomen. There she lays a pod of eggs. All winter long these eggs remain in the ground. Strangely enough, they will not hatch unless the ground has been frozen. In spring, tiny wingless nymphs hatch; it may take them six weeks of greens-eating to reach maturity in colder climates such as New England.

The "Long Horns" Crickets and katydids are easily distinguished from their short-horned cousins by their antennae, which are usually much longer than their body. These "long horns" are the real insect-musicians, singing love songs at night that are more musical and rhythmic than the rasps produced by the leg-wing combination of the short horns. Crickets and katydids use one forewing as a fiddle, and the other as a bow. The warmer the night the more syllables in the song—four, five, or sometimes six. Each syllable is made by one stroke of the wings. The vibrations produced are amplified by the wings themselves, especially by an unveined area in the center of the wing that acts as a sounding board. Their "ears" are tiny oval openings located just below their "knees" on the front legs.

Finding a katydid in the daytime requires very sharp eyes, for it is as green as the leaves it eats, and even the veins of the wings look like leaf veins. The eggs, flat and oval, are laid in overlapping rows on twigs or leaves.

Black field crickets chirp more often during the daytime than their other long-horned relatives. Not exclusively vegetarian, they have been known to eat each other if several are confined in a small space. A female can be distinguished from the male by her long, spear-like ovipositor, which she uses to lay her eggs in the ground, one by one.

Snowy tree crickets—which are actually pale green—are hard to find, even at night when they are singing. Often these insects will form a chorus, singing a high-pitched, two-note song that sounds like *re-treat, re-treat.* This insect has been nicknamed the "temperature cricket," for air temperature in degrees Fahrenheit can be approximated by counting the number of chirps in 15 seconds and then adding 40. The warmer the night, the faster the beat. In the fall, as nights become cooler, the tempo decreases, finally stopping altogether after a sharp frost. The insects succumb to the numbing cold, but their eggs, tucked away on twigs or in the ground, survive to become a new generation of singers the following year.

Springing from its powerful hind legs, the grasshopper jumps up to twenty times its body length. Front and middle legs serve as props and landing gear. The spines of the back legs, rasped against his wings, make "music" to lure his mate.

The female cricket can be distinguished from the male by her long, spearlike ovipositor. With it she lays her eggs in the ground, one by one.

Grasshoppers are called "short horns" because their bodies are longer than their antennae. The wings, which will eventually run the full length of its back, are not yet visible on this nymph. Light reflected from its many lenses causes the compound eye to appear speckled.

The humpbacked camel cricket lives in cellars and other dark, damp places. Unlike most other crickets, it is a meat-eater.

cicadas, hoppers, "ant cows"

Cicadas   Each year in late July, groups of green-eyed monsters tune up to join the insect orchestra. These are the cicadas (si-*kay*-das). Fully an inch long, they look dangerous, but they can neither bite nor sting. A cicada's body is widest at the front, bulging with green compound eyes. When at rest its large transparent green-veined wings are held roof-like over the back. Its long jointed beak is folded under the body when not in use sucking tree sap.

It is the cicadas who make the high-pitched whirring whine you hear from tree tops on hot summer days. The sound is made by a pair of oval-shaped drums on the sides of the abdomen, just behind the base of the hind wings. Each has a membrane stretched tightly across it. As the strong muscles attached to the rim of the drum contract rapidly, they vibrate this membrane. The sound is strongly amplified across the almost hollow, plump abdomen. No other insect can produce sound this way.

But only the male cicadas sing, and they sing to attract females. After mating, the females lay eggs in slits they make on the branches of trees and die soon afterwards. Several weeks later the nymphs hatch and drop to the ground, burrowing in to find tender tree roots. The nymphs live underground for several years, sucking sap from the rootlets, molting and growing, extending their burrows to new roots with mole-like shovels on their front legs. When they are nearly full grown, the nymphs tunnel upward, emerging from the ground on a midsummer evening and climbing partway up a tree trunk or a fence post. There the final molt takes place, the old skeleton splitting down the back. The new pale-green, velvet-winged adult climbs out and hangs quietly for an hour or two while its wings expand and the new armor hardens and darkens. Then, leaving its old brittle skin still hooked to the bark, the cicada continues to climb, finally reaching the treetop by a short flight. There it lives out its brief week or two of adult life.

The cicada is known by other names, all misleading in some way. One is "dog-day harvest fly." Part of the name is true because cicadas are active during the dog-days of August, but technically cicadas are not flies. In the south, cicadas are known as "jar-flies."

The annual cicada's seventeen-year cousin is often called a "locust" but that name should be reserved for the short-horned grasshoppers. This cicada actually does take seventeen years to mature, spending its long adolescence underground. The adult is more slender than the annual cicada, and its eyes and wing veins are red instead of green. It emerges earlier in the year, in late May or early June, and its chirp sounds more mournful. Groups of nymphs mature at the same time, each group being called a "brood." In various areas of New England, there may be several broods maturing at intervals of several years, although each group has taken seventeen years to grow up. Early settlers, observing one such brood, mistook the cicadas for a swarm of locusts, and the name has persisted.

The cicada shell on the left is hollow. The adult on the right has just emerged from it. After feeding on roots as a nymph, the adult will fly up to his new home in the treetops.

In spite of its frightful appearance, this green-eyed monster neither bites nor stings. It is the sapsucking cicada, whose song is heard from treetops on hot summer days.

This view of the cicada's underside reveals a unique feature of its sharp, protruding beak: When not in use it is folded out of the way, under the insect's body. Here it is shown at center, extending downward.

This frothy structure is the home of a spittlebug, or froghopper. The sap from the stalk is used both as food and building material. The nymph remains in this home until it emerges as an adult.

Froghoppers   The time is spring; the place, every field and roadside with tender, sap-filled plants. Here lives the spittlebug, alias the froghopper, a tiny relative of the cicada. It has an enormous appetite for sap, needing it for both food and building material. Both nymphs and adults are sap-tappers, but only the nymph uses built-in bellows to blow a bubble-cluster house around itself.

If you remove the soapy bubble mass, you'll find, in the middle, a pale green gargoyle of an insect, with two dark eyes. If you put it on another part of the plant stalk, you can watch it build more froth to hide in. First, it sinks its beak into the tissue of the plant to the sap tubes, like a new home-owner

If removed from its bubbly home, the froghopper nymph looks fragile and soft-bodied. It will quickly build another house when placed on a juicy stalk.

Froglike in appearance, the adult froghopper even hops like its namesake. Its brown color and full-sized wings indicate that it is full grown.

hooking into the city water supply. On the way through his body the plant sap is changed chemically, waxy substances are added, and the excess fluid emerges, each drop enclosing a bubble of air drawn in through bellows on the insect's underside. Within five or ten minutes it has blown enough bubbles to conceal itself from view.

The bubbles are all about the same size and have amazing staying power, not popping and disappearing gradually as most frothy mixtures do. Only after the nymph has molted for the last time and grown wings does it leave the bubble enclosure. Then it is a drab, tan insect, broad-headed, sometimes al-

The slender leafhopper is vividly banded with red and green. Alone, this tiny sapsucker is not very formidable. But together with others of its kind — sometimes as many as a million to an acre — it causes great damage to plants.

Dark brown and humpbacked, the treehopper is most frequently found on forest trees. It breeds but one generation per year, and the adult does not appear until late summer.

most as wide as it is long. When it squats on a plant stem it does look rather froglike. It can even hop, too.

Leafhoppers   These tiny sapsuckers, because of sheer numbers—as many as a million to an acre—can cause a tremendous amount of damage to plants. The stiletto beak of each leafhopper is tiny, the drop of sap it extracts is barely noticeable, but if dozens are feeding on the same plant, they remove enough sap to make the plant droop and slow growth. In the course of feeding, leafhoppers can also

Aphids — plant lice — feed on plant sap in colonies. Often they remove so much sap that the part of the plant above them dies.

A whole colony of aphids bores into a plant stem. When the stalk becomes too crowded, the winged adult will fly to another plant.

introduce virus diseases to plants, so their activities can have damaging economic consequences.

Leafhoppers are slender insects with pointed heads. Only three-eighths of an inch long, they are vividly striped with red and green or blue. They are very active, snapping away violently as soon as you come near them or try to pick them up. Leafhoppers can fly as well as hop—in some parts of the country they are aptly called "dodgers."

Their cousins, the treehoppers, have been nicknamed the "brownies of the insect world." Each kind has a distinctive body shape, with the thorax greatly enlarged to form a long horn or sail or knob. Some look like thorns, and for

29

that reason are often overlooked by birds. Inhabiting trees rather than field plants, treehoppers are either solid brown or green in color. There is only one generation a year, and the adults usually do not appear until August.

Aphids   An astonishing method of speeding up their reproductive rate is responsible for the success of aphids as a group. Instead of the usual pattern of egg,

Cone-shaped aphid galls protrude from this witch hazel leaf. These tissue growths provide both home and food for the young aphids. They are always open on the underside, permitting their inhabitants to come and go.

nymph, and adult, the still-immature summer nymphs are able to produce young without mating. Each nymph produces eggs which are kept in its body until they are ready to hatch, so the nymph appears to give birth to living young. Each nymph can produce up to four young a day, each of which needs about ten days of growth to be able to do the same thing. In this way, as many as thirteen generations may be produced each season.

Not surprisingly, aphids are a scourge to gardeners, who call them plant lice. Not only do they reproduce quickly, but they also come in infinite variety. Eight thousand species are known, and they can be any color of the rainbow—white or cream-colored, pale or bright yellow, pink, red, blue-green, light or dark green, purple, brown, black, or gray. Some are solid colored; some are spotted. Some are woolly. They are all very small—their pear-shaped bodies are scarcely a tenth of an inch long.

Some winged aphids are produced in each generation—the number increases as winter approaches. It is not known whether or not light and/or crowding has any influence on the production of winged forms. When aphids become too crowded on a plant, winged forms disperse to other plants to begin a new colony. True male and female forms do not appear until the temperature drops in the fall. Then aphids mate and lay eggs that will winter on the bark of trees. Aphid eggs, too, are numerous.

The aphid has many enemies. In one chickadee stomach 450 aphid eggs were found, the result of one day's searching of bark crevices. Birds are not aphids' only enemies, however, for daddy-long-legs, as well as both larval and adult forms of the lacewing fly and lady beetle eat them avidly, and syrphid flies and tiny wasps parasitize them.

However, the aphid has at least one friend. Cornfield ants store aphid eggs in underground galleries over the winter, and when the aphid nymphs hatch in spring they are taken to tender young corn plants. There the aphid nymphs feed on the plant sap. During the summer, these "ant cows" can be "milked" of a sweet secretion, called honeydew, by the ants. When necessary the ant "cowboys" move their prize aphid herds to juicier plants, all the while enjoying the rich honeydew.

Aphids are serious plant pests. They can cause abnormal growths of tissue called galls on many plants—on elm and witch-hazel leaves, grape vines, and blue spruce twigs. They can destroy many plants because there are so many tiny beaks sucking sap. They can also transmit plant diseases.

Another member of the sapsucking clan is the scale insect. Orchards are host to myriads of these minute, hard-to-control pests. All scale insects are not destructive, however. Shellac is obtained from a scale insect native to India, and waxes and dyes come from other tropical scales. These few members of the order of clear wings help to tip the balance away from complete destructiveness.

x marks the bug

To most people, any small many-legged creature is a "bug." But the name should not be used indiscriminately. Stinkbugs, bed bugs and squash bugs are all true bugs. Lightningbugs, ladybugs, sowbugs, spittlebugs, and June bugs are not.

All bugs belong to one particular order of the insect family. The distinguishing characteristic is very simple: when you look at a stinkbug, for example, you can see clearly across its back a diagonal X that marks it as a true bug. This effect is produced by the texture of the wings and the way they are arranged. The basal half of each forewing is leathery and opaque, while the tip is thin and transparent. At rest, the bug folds these wings with the thin tips overlapping. True bugs belong to the order Hemiptera, which means "half-wing." So remember, X marks the bug.

All bugs make their living by sucking liquids through a sharp, jointed beak. Some live on plants and suck the sap, while others live in ponds, capturing other insects and draining them of their juices. A few bugs, namely the bed bug and its close relatives, live on the blood of larger animals, such as people, bats, or birds.

Plant Bugs Because they eat upward from the underside of leaves, most plant bugs do their damage unseen. If they do happen to be on the upper side of a leaf, they are quick to scuttle out of sight if there is any movement near the plant. As a result, there is probably a much larger population of plant bugs than a gardener may be aware of. His only clue may be rusty, dead-looking spots on the leaves where sucking beaks have interfered with sap circulation. But don't blame bugs for the holes you may find in the leaves. Bugs have only piercing mouthparts. They have no jaws, and cannot nibble leaves at all.

Carnivorous ambush bugs and assassin bugs use plants as decoys. They much prefer animal juices to pallid plant sap. They lie in wait on a flower, often one that matches them in color, until another insect happens by, attracted by nectar or pollen. With a lunge, the bug captures and holds its victim with its strong front claws. Then it sinks its sharp beak in and sucks the insect dry. Apparently a digestive fluid is injected to liquefy the prey. The bug's beak is sharp enough to penetrate human skin and can inflict a painful bite, probably because of the chemicals that are injected.

Stinkbugs live up to their name. Many plant bugs can produce unpleasant odors by means of special glands in the thorax, but the stinkbug outdoes them all. This may be a defensive action, keeping birds and other predators from eating as many as they might. Stinkbugs are rather large for bugs—almost a half-inch long. They are wide-shouldered and shield-shaped, often brightly-colored. One common type is a vivid green.

Smaller and narrower in body are certain bugs named for the particular plant they prefer as food, such as the bronzed squash bug and the gaudy orange and black milkweed bug.

This assassin bug waits on a flower for an insect to be attracted by the nectar or pollen. Then these long, spined claws will snatch the victim, and the sharp beak will suck its blood.

The assassin bug's long beak folds back under its curiously elongated head. Through this beak he injects digestive juices into the prey, then sucks up the liquefied food. After his meal he drops the empty insect skin.

As its name suggests, the stink bug smells. Special glands in its thorax produce the odor, possibly as a protection against enemies. Shieldlike in shape, it is often a vivid green color.

The Miridae, a large family of brightly marked bugs having no common names, feed on a variety of plants. One of these, often seen in early summer, is striped with black and brilliant green.

The lace bug's beautiful texture shows up best when magnified, for it is only an eighth of an inch long. While it may appear to be delicate and fragile-looking, it can be very destructive when large numbers attack the undersides of leaves.

Grasses, whether grown for crops or in lawns, are the special province of the quarter-inch-long chinch bug, a serious pest with black body, white wings, and red legs.

The "X", which stands out on the back of the milkweed bug, identifies it as a true bug. The "X" is formed by the crossed position in which the bug rests its wings.

Many water bugs can inflict painful wounds if they are carelessly handled. But first they have to be caught, and this isn't easy. Fringed legs, flattened and oarlike, enable water bugs to swim a fast retreat if threatened. By the same token they're a good match for the lively prey they stalk.

In spite of the fact that they live in ponds, water bugs are all air breathers. They must surface periodically to renew their oxygen supply, carrying it down into the water with them in special ways. At the surface, a water boatman traps bubbles of air under its wings and on body hairs, then swims jerkily down. The backswimmer carries air in grooves on the underside of the abdomen. This makes his underside lighter, so he is forced to swim upside down, his buoyant abdomen gleaming silver.

Long and stick-like, the two-inch water scorpion has a long breathing tube at the end of its abdomen. It is not as active as most other water bugs, so between surface trips—with the inch-long breathing tube just dimpling the surface—it clings to underwater stems to wait for its dinner, relying on its resemblance to a dead twig to conceal it.

All of these water bugs are predatory, capturing other small aquatic creatures and sucking their juices. The larger they are, the larger their prey. The giant water bug, often two inches long and shaped like a huge watermelon seed, is strong enough to subdue tadpoles and even small fish. As a matter of fact, giant water bugs can be a serious problem in a fish hatchery if they are abundant. They are strong flyers, too. At night they are attracted by lights, so many people know them as "electric light bugs."

Wings may seem unnecessary equipment for bugs that spend so much time underwater, but they are an advantage if a pond happens to dry up during the summer. The winged adults can fly to other ponds and thus survive.

Walking on water is quite a feat, but water striders do it. They skim along on the surface of quiet water, with their slight weight well distributed by the six long and widely spaced legs. Each hairy leg then merely dimples the water and there is not enough weight in any one spot to break through the surface tension. Darting rapidly about, sometimes even hopping, water striders feed mostly on insects that have fallen onto the surface of the water and are too wet to escape. Sometimes they capture insects coming to the surface for air. The water strider is one of the very few insects at home on salt water. It lives in the Sargasso Sea, an enormous floating mat of seaweed in the Atlantic Ocean, a thousand miles from land.

Adult bugs usually hibernate during the winter, either in the leaf litter on the ground if they are plant bugs, or in the mud of pond bottoms if they are water bugs. Only after they emerge in spring do they lay eggs, which hatch in short order. There may be only one generation a year for many bugs. The nymphs grow up gradually, finally attaining wings when they are adult.

The tiny lace bug is frequently overlooked, for it is barely an eighth of an inch long and feeds on the undersides of leaves. But its beauty is readily seen when this flat, textured bug is greatly magnified.

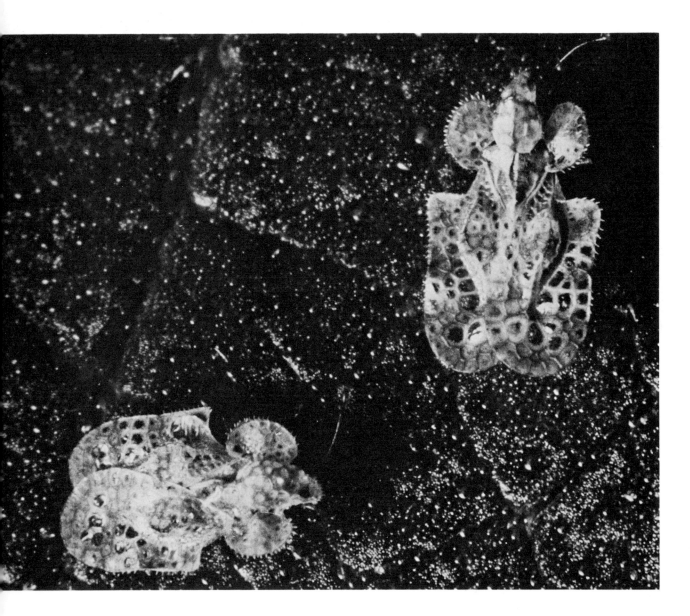

The sticklike water scorpion, clinging to an underwater plant stem, thrusts its breathing tube through the surface film of the water. This way it breathes in comfort while waiting for a victim to swim within its grasp.

dragons and damsels

Dragonflies have a reputation for being dangerous. They are called "horse stingers" and "devil's darning needles." As a child you may remember being told that dragonflies "sew up the ears of bad little boys." But in truth, dragonflies are not in the least dangerous to people. They have no stinger or any other insidious equipment to harm us. On the contrary, they are a great help. By eating great numbers of midges, mosquitoes, and flies, they cut down the number of potential human bites.

Dragonflies live in and for flight. They may pursue, catch, and eat their food; mate; lay their eggs; and elude their enemies while airborne. They have two equal pairs of narrow wings, a long narrow abdomen which offers little air resistance, and slender legs which bristle with stiff hairs. The legs, which are never used for walking, are carried well forward, held like a basket to capture and hold small insects to be eaten in flight.

At first glance a dragonfly's head seems to be all eyes. The jaws underneath and the antennae are completely overshadowed by the impressive visual equipment. Most apparent are two bulging compound eyes which almost meet on top. Each of these eyes is actually a complex of some 30,000 individual lenses. But that's not all. In a small triangle on the front of the head are three more eyes. These are the simple single-lens eyes used to distinguish light from dark.

The enormous globular compound eyes dominate. Each is like a curved honeycomb, made up of rows and rows of hexagonal cells. Each cell is cone-shaped, with a lens at the surface, narrowing down to a fiber leading to the optic nerve. There is no pupil or iris or retina, as in human beings, nor is there any focussing mechanism. Instead, the insect probably senses a mosaic of dots, somewhat like a newspaper picture seen under a magnifying glass—a pattern of light and dark. When a moving object crosses the field of vision, lens after lens is stimulated and the insect becomes aware of motion. The size and speed of the object determines how many and how fast successive lenses are stimulated. This information directs the insect's flight pattern: something small probably means food, so the insect flies toward it; something large means danger, so the insect will fly away.

With eyes so big and complex it is not surprising that the dragonfly can notice movement in almost every direction: in front, to each side, above and below. The rear view, however, is blocked by the dragonfly's long abdomen. This is its Achilles' heel, and hence the best way to catch a dragonfly is to approach it from the rear.

The dragonfly has an enormous appetite, putting it in a class with the most voracious insects of all: the praying mantis and the robber fly. In only two hours the dragonfly can eat its weight in flies. Further, if the dragonfly is imprisoned without food, its insatiable hunger will not stop at self-cannibalism: it will begin eating the end of its abdomen.

Dragonflies cruise at twenty-four miles per hour, but they can go as fast as thirty-six miles per hour in short bursts. They can also rapidly change

Dragonflies live in and for flight. In the air they eat, mate, and lay their eggs. They cruise at twenty-four miles per hour, capturing mosquitoes and flies along the way.

The dragonfly nymph is as much a master under water, as shown in this photograph, as the adult is in the air. Its color blends in with the mud and debris, and special gills extract oxygen from the water. To capture its food, the nymph shoots out its hooked lower lip. It then draws the victim back into its mouth.

This photo captures a rare moment of action: For the last time this dragonfly breaks out from an old skin beneath it. The gleaming contorted shape will soon change as its wings expand and dry in the air. Then its airborne adult life will begin.

course—darting here, swooping there, or perhaps just hovering, helicopter-fashion, in mid-air. No other insect can match this kind of speed and maneuverability. Often a dragonfly will patrol a beat along the edge of a pond, just like a policeman, returning now and then to a perch—perhaps a twig jutting out over the water—to munch a newly caught insect. But apparently dragonflies are sun-worshippers. When a cloud passes over the sun, the dragonfly stops flying and perches until the sun comes out again. Dragonflies are not in evidence on overcast days.

In the fall an alert observer can see groups of dragonflies or even single ones flying southwest—the same direction that Monarch butterflies follow. Whether dragonflies are also migrating is still a question, but their movements at this time of year are certainly suggestive. Perhaps some do travel south, avoiding the cold death that would await them in late fall.

When a cloud shadows the sun, the dragonfly perches on the end of a twig. It will not fly if the sky is overcast. Even when the insect is at rest, its wings remain outstretched.

More slender and delicate than the robust dragonfly nymph, the damselfly nymph also spends its youth under water. The three finlike tails are gills, with which the insect breathes.

Growing Up   Many kinds of dragonflies mate in flight. Then they dip the tips of their abdomens into ponds, washing off the eggs, which soon settle to the bottom. When the nymph hatches, it is an ugly duckling—wide, awkward, and unattractive. Yet—like the adult—it is extremely talented in its own way. The adult is a master hunter in air; the nymph is a master in water.

The nymph dragonfly breathes by means of internal gills and so never

Bulging compound eyes and a built-in insect net characterize the adult damselfly, shown here. In flight it uses these six hairy legs like a basket. Insects that come near the stiff bristles are easy prey.

needs to surface for air. The gills are located in a cavity at the end of the abdomen. Oxygen is absorbed from water as it is drawn past the gills. In times of danger, water can be swiftly ejected from this cavity, enabling the nymph to jet forward, escaping its enemy in the cloud of mud that is stirred up.

Most of the time the debris-colored nymph skulks or stalks along the pond bottom hunting for food. When a likely insect or tiny fish comes within range, the nymph's magnificent mouth structure comes into play. This is a long, hinged lower lip, with hooks at the end. It folds back innocently under the head when not in use, but springs out lethally—five times the length of the head—when prey is near.

Depending on the species, this kind of life continues for a period of one, two, or three years with ten to fifteen molts. Finally, when the wing pads have increased enough in size, early on a morning between May and September, the nymph leaves the water and climbs out on the stem of a plant growing in the shallows. There, hidden by the leaves of the plant, the nymph transforms into the adult simply by shedding its split nymph skin and clinging to the plant stem while its wings expand and dry. This is a time of danger, for the dragon-fly cannot move until its wings are dry and ready to operate. In this helpless state they are easy prey for frogs or herons.

Damselflies Smaller, more slender-bodied and delicate-looking damselflies have habits of flight that contrast strongly with those of the dragonfly. Damselflies fly feebly, always low, and often flit, butterflylike, perching frequently on leaves or twigs near the water. Their wing position at rest is different, too, and an easy way to separate them from dragonflies: damselflies hold their wings together over their backs, like sails, but dragonflies can never fold their wings. They are permanently outstretched, like the wings of an airplane. Many common dam-selflies have brilliantly colored abdomens, metallic blues and greens and violets that often fade when the insect dies.

On bright summer days, mated pairs of damselflies often fly in tandem over ponds. The eggs are laid in plant tissues, underwater, and while diving under is not too difficult, damselflies have a hard time breaking through the surface film to leave the water again. Both struggle to get the male out, and then he tows the female out by flying desperately upward.

Damselfly nymphs mature more quickly than dragonflies. Sometimes there are two broods a year. These nymphs are carnivores also, and have the same kind of jointed lower lip for capturing prey, but they have external gills for breathing: three filamentous finlike appendages at the end of the abdomen. They sometimes swim by using these gill-tails as oars. When the right time comes, they too climb out on plant stems, just above the water, to become adults. Sometimes dozens of empty nymph skins may coat plant stems around the edges of a pond.

scale wings

A butterfly seems to have no responsibilities in life. Leisurely, delicately, it flits from flower to flower in the sunshine, gracefully free from drudgery.

But the butterfly's life is not as carefree as it seems. The female has a job to do. She must find the right kind of plant on which to lay her eggs, so that the hatching caterpillars will have the proper food available. As the butterfly visits plant after plant, she tests them for flavor, tasting the chemicals in the leaf with sensitive hairs on her feet. Only when she finds the right kind of plant will she glue her eggs to it. Because she can fly, she is able to range widely in her search.

Some kinds of butterflies lay only one egg on a leaf; others attach a cluster of eggs. The eggs are difficult to find because they are so small, but they are fascinating when magnified, varying in shape, color, and surface markings. Soon—within a few days if the weather is warm—the wormlike caterpillar hatches from the egg.

Worm or Caterpillar? To many people, any creature that crawls and has a soft, tubular body is a worm. But caterpillars have features no worms have. A worm cannot see, but the caterpillar can distinguish light from dark with several minute eyes on each side of its head. A worm has no jaws, but the caterpillar has very efficient mouthparts called mandibles that work sideways. A worm has no legs, but a caterpillar has two kinds, and several pairs of each: each of three segments behind the caterpillar's head has a pair of slender jointed legs, equipped with claws to grip the leaf surface as it chews. Farther back, along the abdomen, there are five pairs of thick fleshy legs, each with a circle of tiny hooklets around its large base. These wide prolegs provide good support for the weight of the long abdomen. The hooklets also help the caterpillar cling to plant surfaces. Finally, the worm will never change shape when it matures. It will always be a blind, legless, jawless creature.

In addition to structural differences, caterpillars and worms also do different things. For example, caterpillars can make silk—a talent no worm can equal. Produced by silk glands located in the head, the liquid silk is extruded through an opening in the lower lip and hardens when it is exposed to the air.

This silk is used by caterpillars for many different purposes: leaf rollers and tiers use silk to tack leaves together, forming a shelter; tent caterpillars spin paths of silk on twigs wherever they go, and build community webs; inchworms spin out a lifeline of silk and drop from it when a bird jostles the branch on which they are feeding. Then, when all is quiet again, the inchworm climbs back up the lifeline, eating the silk as it goes. Some, but not all moths, use silk for making cocoons. Only one kind of caterpillar spins a single long thread that can be unwound easily from the cocoon without breaking. This is the Oriental silk moth caterpillar, misnamed "silk-worm." It is native to China, and has been domesticated by man for centuries.

How to Keep
from Being Eaten
Besides spinning protective tents, or lifelines, some caterpillars can also ward off enemies by making noises, giving off unpleasant odors, or using color patterns to warn enemies or camouflage themselves as they go about their only business of eating.

To frighten away hungry birds, the Sphinx moth caterpillar squeaks, and the Mourning Cloak can make a faint grating or buzzing sound. The Polyphemus larva, a large caterpillar, clicks its jaws audibly.

The Black Swallowtail is the skunk of the caterpillar world. When it is disturbed, a bright orange forked "horn" emerges from an opening just behind the head, and emits a disagreeable smell.

Fake eyespots are the weapon the Tiger Swallowtail caterpillar uses in its psychological warfare, while bright vivid stripes, denoting bitter flavor, are the Monarch caterpillar's means of defense. Generally speaking, the thick fuzzy coats of some caterpillars are in themselves a useful deterrent, limiting predators to those few birds that don't mind hairy food. A few caterpillars, including the Io moth and the Saddleback, have hairs that produce itching or a rash on contact. Some caterpillars depend on color to hide them, blending with their backgrounds as the Cabbage caterpillars do, and others imitate twigs by becoming rigid when disturbed. Still other caterpillars sport all manner of fancy tubercles, branched spines or horns, which probably look distasteful.

Caterpillars need all the defenses they can muster. They must concentrate on eating, and eating is really all they are equipped for. Each kind of caterpillar is a food specialist. Some, like the Monarch caterpillar, eat only one kind of plant; in this case milkweed leaves are the choice. Since milkweed is not found in Europe, neither are Monarchs. Other kinds of caterpillars will feed on the leaves of any member of one plant family: the Cabbage butterfly will accept cabbage, cauliflower, or broccoli leaves, all relatives. A few caterpillars are less fastidious and don't mind eating any of several food plants, although one is usually the favorite. The tent caterpillar can be found on a number of forest and shade trees, though it usually lives on the wild cherry.

The sculptured egg of the monarch butterfly is smaller than the head of a pin. Each egg is glued individually to the underside of a milkweed leaf. After hatching, the caterpillar eats the eggshell first, then begins to chew on the plant.

Caterpillars vary widely in their eating habits. Some devour the whole leaf down to the midrib. Others eat only the tender portions of leaf tissue between the veins, thus skeletonizing the leaf. Some caterpillars, the leaf miners, are so small that they live inside a leaf, eating the middle green layer and making a colorless serpentine track or a circular white blotch on the leaf.

Similar to other immature insect forms, the caterpillar must molt periodically. Each time, the old skin splits on the back behind the head, and the caterpillar crawls out, leaving the skin shriveled and empty.

After each molt, the caterpillar may look different, changing color or pattern or other details. Since there are seven hundred species of butterflies and seven thousand species of moths in the United States, each of which may molt five times as a caterpillar, with a possible change in appearance each time, identification becomes rather complicated. If you want to find out what kind of caterpillar you've seen, the easiest thing to do would be to raise it (keeping it supplied with fresh leaves from the kind of plant it was on), and let it develop into an adult. Naming it then will be much easier.

Viewed head-on, the monarch caterpillar is vividly banded with orange, black, and white. Two pairs of whiplike extensions add to its unique appearance.

Attached to a spot of silk, a full-grown monarch caterpillar hangs from a plant stalk. In this curved position it waits for internal changes to begin. Soon it will shed its striped skin for the last time.

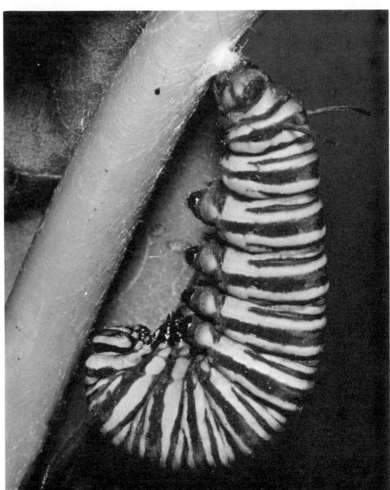

While it hangs from the same spot, its outer skin hardens into a beautiful turquoise case. Inside this pupa case, the larva changes into a butterfly.

Shortly before the adult butterfly is ready to emerge, the walls of the case become transparent. Through them the brilliantly colored adult can be seen.

Head first, the mature butterfly emerges from its pupa case. Behind it the transparent skin still clings to the leaf.

Crumpled and wet, the newborn adult climbs out of its former home, or chrysalis.

The Caterpillar Grows Up

Our body shape is much the same when we are young and when we are grown, but a caterpillar changes radically in form and habit when it reaches adulthood. The caterpillar's main function is eating. It has chewing jaws, a digestive system that can handle the tremendous quantity of food eaten, and legs that serve well for supporting the long abdomen and holding on to a leaf. There is no unnecessary equipment.

The adult's prime function is reproduction. Its job is to find a mate and lay eggs on the proper kinds of plants. The adult has wings that enable it to make its search widely and easily. Eating is of minor importance; an adult may not eat at all. Some large silk moths never eat as adults; they have no mouthparts or digestive system. Their adult lives are very brief, a matter of days at the most. They live long enough to mate and lay eggs. Energy for their activity comes from the food eaten by the caterpillar. Those adults that do eat are on a liquid diet, siphoning nectar from flowers through a long tongue which is kept coiled when not in use.

54

The butterfly must now expand his wings completely before they harden in the air. Otherwise, they will set in a cramped, distorted shape, and the insect will be unable to fly.

Wings outstretched, this new monarch butterfly is ready to fly. The vivid colors are actually layers of scales on the wings. Underneath, the wings themselves are transparent.

The distinguishing features of the moth are shown by this side view of the female cecropia
—a plump, furry body and feathery, ornate "feelers." Butterflies, on the other hand, have
smooth, slender bodies and simple antennae.

When the caterpillar has reached full size, a strange set of changes takes place, triggered by the release of certain hormones. Feeding ceases, and the caterpillar may wander from its plant home to find a place suitable for the transformation. This may be underground, or inside a silken cocoon, or perhaps suspended from a twig.

After a motionless period of a day or two, the caterpillar sheds its old skin for the last time, and becomes a pupa. Its body is now both reminiscent of the caterpillar that was, and suggestive of the adult to be, with wings and antennae outlined.

During the pupa stage the caterpillar tissues dissolve, and from them, new adult organs for flight, sensation, and reproduction are formed. This is complete metamorphosis, a complete change in body form with its corresponding change in function. Caterpillar organs that would be useless to the adult liquefy and are reorganized into tissue that will be useful to the adult.

Jaws disappear, and a tube-tongue forms (or no mouthparts at all). Compound eyes that can detect motion develop, as well as antennae whose function will be to hear and smell. Two pairs of wings, which began an inward growth during the caterpillar stage, now turn outward and develop further. Muscles to work the new wings begin to form. The jointed legs lengthen and develop sensory hairs that are capable of tasting, while the fat prolegs disappear. Reproductive organs form, making fertilization and egg-laying possible.

During this stage of transformation, the creature is not lifeless. It still requires air and some moisture, and when it is touched it responds by moving. But it is totally defenseless. It may be eaten by predators such as mice or birds, or the pupa may be consumed by internal parasites developing from eggs that were laid on the caterpillar. Often the pupa serves as food for these developing parasites and the moth or butterfly never does develop.

But if all goes well, the adult insect emerges, fully formed, but strangely telescoped, for the wings are folded, soft, and crumpled. Now it needs a place with room enough for the wings to unfurl and spread wide. As blood is pumped into them, they begin to expand and harden in the air. If there is not enough room, the wings will harden while they are still crumpled and the insect will never fly.

Moth or | There are no easy ways to tell moths from butterflies during the first three
Butterfly? | stages of their lives—as eggs, caterpillars, or pupae—but the adults differ in several ways. Butterflies usually have simple antennae with knobbed tips, while moths have feathery, ornate "feelers." If the insect's body is slender and rather smooth, it is a butterfly; moths have plump, furry bodies. Butterflies rest with their wings folded together above the back looking like a sail, but moths spread their wings flat when at rest. Finally, most butterflies are active only during daylight hours, while most moths begin to fly at dusk.

This half-inch egg cluster is weatherproofed by a coat of "varnish." In early April the tiny tent caterpillars inside will hatch and chew on the new spring leaves.

Wherever it goes, the tent caterpillar leaves a path of silk. Each member of the colony also helps spin the community shelter, which is enlarged as the colony grows.

Tent caterpillars eat and sleep in large numbers. Attacking together, this fuzzy group may soon finish these partially gnawed leaves.

The silk shelter of the tent caterpillar firmly stretches between branches of a wild cherry tree. When new it is a beautiful structure; later it often becomes torn by birds or stained by rain and droppings.

Long hairs protect the tent caterpillar from hungry birds. When fully grown it may be two and a half inches long. Then it will crawl from the colony and seek a solitary place to pupate.

The tent caterpillar may weave its loose cocoon almost anywhere — under window ledges, along the rim of a tire, or like this one, among the leaves on the forest floor. In a week or two the adult will emerge.

Moths and butterflies belong to the order Lepidoptera, which means "scale wings." Lepidoptera wings are covered with rows of scales which overlap each other like shingles on a roof. If you should touch a moth or butterfly wing some "dust" would rub off on your fingers. These are the scales. Remove enough of them and you will find transparent wings underneath, for it is the scales that give the wings their color.

Variations on a Theme All moths and butterflies have basically the same life cycle: egg, larva, pupa, adult. They begin life as eggs laid on the food plant, then they hatch from the egg in caterpillar form and begin to eat voraciously. Reaching full size, they are ready to pupate, and transform into the winged adult whose function it is to lay eggs.

Each kind of moth or butterfly follows this pattern of growth but each has its own variations, from shape of egg to favorite food plant, color and markings as a caterpillar, and pattern and habit as an adult. The length of time that each of the four life stages requires varies too, the rate of development increasing with increasing temperature.

Inside the cocoon the pupa looks lifeless and defenseless. But if touched, it will respond by wriggling. Antennae of the adult moth are outlined at the left of the pupa skin.

White stripes span the wings of the adult tent caterpillar. This is a female; the male, equally furry, is smaller and has larger antennae.

Sphinx moths, also known as hawk moths, have large bodies and long, pointed wings. Because of their size and habit of hovering over flowers, they are often mistaken for hummingbirds.

Of course, all insects are inactive outdoors during the winter. Moths and butterflies may spend the cold months in any of the four stages, depending on the species: tent caterpillars spend the winter as eggs, woolly bears hibernate as caterpillars, and silk moths as pupae inside their silk cocoons. Mourning Cloaks hibernate as adults, while Monarch adults migrate south in the fall, and another generation returns north in the late spring.

At close range, the sphinx moth's head looks well combed. When disturbed the sphinx caterpillar raises the front of its two-inch body and draws its head under.

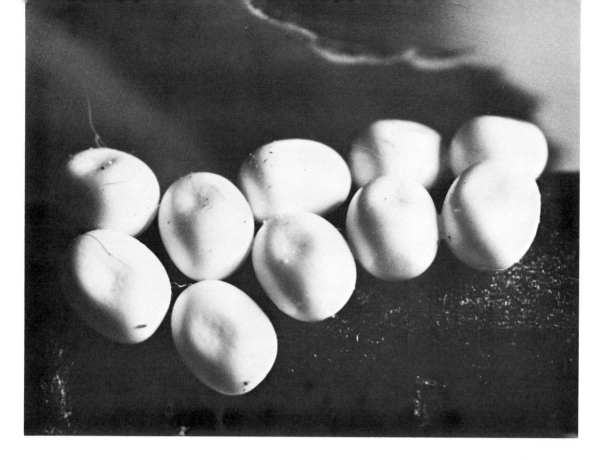

The promethea moth lays its smooth, white eggs in a cluster. Each slightly larger than the head of a pin, they are frequently found on spicebush leaves.

Almost full grown, this pale green promethea moth caterpillar emerges from its skin for the last time. Splitting first at the thorax, the old skin moves back along the abdomen as its occupant wiggles out.

Two pairs of large red protuberances decorate the thorax of the promethea larva, while six rows of small black knobs dot the rest of its body. At the right, partly bent under, is the caterpillar's head.

All caterpillars have three pairs of legs on the thorax which become the six legs of the adult. Most caterpillars also have five pairs of temporary legs to support their long abdomens. But the inchworm has only two pairs, as shown here on the left. Therefore, it must loop along by moving first its back set of legs, then its front set.

From this buckled position the inchworm will extend the front part of its body. Then it will loop again by crawling forward on its back legs.

The inchworm spins no cocoon. Its naked pupa hides in the leaf litter under the tree where it grew up. From this shell will emerge either a male moth with tan inch-wide wings or a wingless female.

Because the adult mourning cloak hibernates during cold weather, it is often the earliest butterfly to appear. Occasionally on a warm day in February it can be seen flying around sunny spots in the woods.

The scraggly head of the mourning cloak is covered with an abundance of hair. Even its compound eye looks hairy.

Sometimes the adult moth or butterfly never leaves its pupa case. Instead, it is devoured by a parasite, such as the wasp that emerged from this cocoon and left the original pupa case hanging from the exit. The wasp grew up by feeding on the mourning cloak that lived there.

A colony of wasp larvae drew their food from the body of this hornworm. Shown here in the cocoon stage, they remain on the host's back. The hornworm will not live much longer — its tissues have been eaten away by the parasitic larvae.

true flies

Male mosquitoes never bite. It is the female who is the culprit. She bites because she needs a meal of blood so that her eggs will develop. To get this liquid food she pierces your skin with a complex array of lances, six in all, which are enclosed in a sheath. Before any blood can be withdrawn through this very narrow tube, the mosquito injects a chemical which will keep the blood from clotting while she pumps. This is why a mosquito bite itches, for the anticoagulant is irritating. If she is a particular kind of mosquito that has recently sucked blood from a person who has malaria or yellow fever, she may be harboring in her salivary glands the microorganisms that cause these diseases, and may inject some of them into a healthy person along with her anti-clot material. But some kinds of mosquitoes can bite without producing an itch. Sometimes a mosquito may miss a capillary and get no food.

Males never transmit disease since they do not bite. But they too live on a liquid diet, sucking nectar from flowers or juices from ripe fruit. In order to locate the whining females, male mosquitoes are equipped with ornate, feathery antennae which are tuned to the high-pitched song of their female. Since females do not need to hear, their antennae are not so much like plumes, but they are still sensitive in other ways. Their antennae are used to locate potential victims by odor and temperature.

Mosquitoes live in water during the early stages of their lives. The eggs float on the surface, either singly or in rafts. Legless larvae called "wrigglers" breathe through long air tubes attached to the ends of their bodies. Feeding on microscopic plants and animals abundant in standing water, the larvae grow quickly, soon becoming big-headed pupae. Two air tubes on the thorax enable the pupa to breathe when it is at the surface. In fact, an easy way to eliminate mosquitoes is to pour a film of oil on the water surface, making it impossible for either the larvae or pupae to breathe. But mosquitoes at all stages of development have many natural predators. Fish and frogs eat enormous numbers of young mosquitoes as well as adults. Dragonflies, swallows, and bats devour many others.

Adult mosquitoes, like midges and gnats, crane flies and house flies, have only two wings. Short knobbed projections called "halteres" replace the

73

Dangling upside down below the surface of the water, the mosquito larva breathes through a tube on the end of its abdomen. It feeds on microscopic plants and animals.

second pair of wings. They are balancing organs which act like gyroscopes, vibrating rapidly in opposition to the wing beat. When the wings move up, the halteres move down. If one or both halteres is removed, the insect can no longer fly. It sideslips and yaws, out of control. In people, this sense of balance derives from structures in the inner ear. If something goes wrong with this mechanism, a person has difficulty in navigating, and even standing up. Halteres perform the same function for true flies.

The halteres make the flight of a fly very maneuverable. Some, such as the yellow-banded flower fly, can fly backward as well as forward, hover in one spot, and even fly upside down. Wingbeat is extremely rapid, often as fast as three hundred beats a second.

Flies also have large compound eyes. They can easily detect motion—a factor which explains why they are so hard to catch. Some flies are also very

In spite of its mosquitolike appearance, the inch-long cranefly does not bite. Behind its wings are two knobby projections. These balancing organs, or halteres, replace the back wings on all true flies.

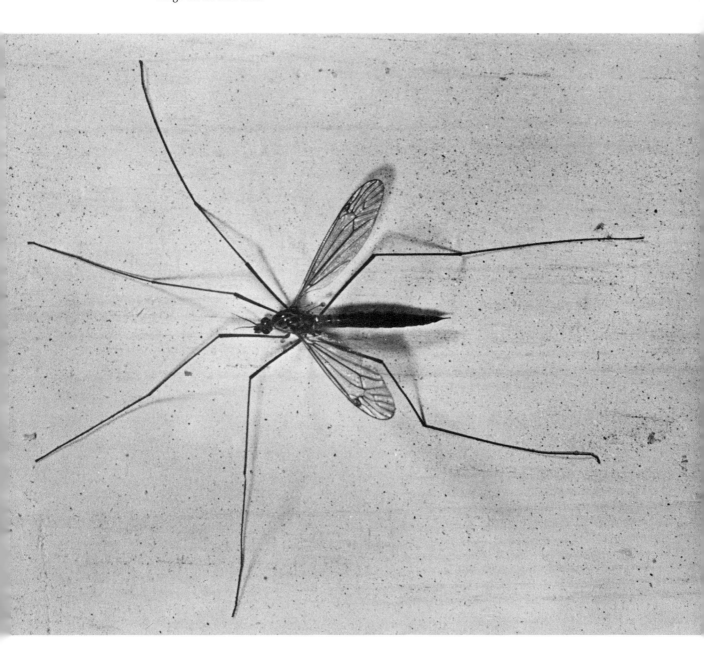

Many fly larvae, or maggots, are helpful scavengers because they eat the decaying flesh of dead animals. Here, a blowfly lays its eggs on a piece of rotting meat.

swift in flight. Deer flies, for example, well known for their painful bites, can travel as fast as a horse can gallop.

The larvae of all true flies are legless, blind, groping creatures, wide at the back and tapering toward the front. They move by alternately stretching and contracting. Some larvae seem headless. They protrude an extensible proboscis when food is near, using it to suck the juices. All fly larvae are known as maggots. They are all meateaters, exuding chemicals that predigest the food, and then absorbing it as a liquid. The larvae of the syrphid fly lives on aphids, helping to keep that population in control. Doctors have deliberately put the carnivorous habits of some larvae to work cleaning up dead or dying tissue around wounds. Many flies are scavengers, being attracted to decaying flesh by the odor. Adults lay eggs in such places, and the maggots make short work of the meat, converting it rapidly into fly tissue.

Crane flies frighten many people because they look so much like giant mosquitoes, but they cannot bite. Some have bodies an inch long, and their single pair of narrow wings can also measure an inch. Because of their size, their knobbed halteres are easily seen. Six extremely long slender legs complete the picture. These legs break off easily, so seeing a crane fly with five legs or fewer is not unusual. It has simply saved its life by sacrificing a leg.

Swarms of crane flies are common in damp areas, where they often dance up and down in the air. They are not strong flyers, moving only slowly and for short distances in the air. Fishermen call the adults "spinners," and use them as models for dry flies. (All dry flies are imitation winged insects; wet flies are patterned after underwater fish food such as larvae, nymphs, pupae, and minnows.)

Some crane fly larvae are aquatic, but most kinds live in the ground, feeding on dead plants. A few eat the roots of living plants. The tough brown skin of these larvae gives them the name of "leather-jackets."

Black flies are a hazard for fishermen or campers near swift streams in spring. Adults are small, humpbacked, and black, with big round eyes. They fly swiftly. Bites are painful, sometimes causing swelling, and often continuing to bleed for hours. The larvae live in groups on rocks in the stream, clinging tightly with suction discs at the end of their bodies, and gorging themselves on microscopic plant and animal life. To move safely in the rapids, they spin guy lines of silk and follow them. The pupa stage takes place under water too. Air is extracted by gills from the water, and forms a bubble under the pupal skin. When the adult is ready to emerge, it pops up to the surface in this bubble of air, and flies away.

The house fly does not bite. Instead of having a piercing proboscis, its mouthparts are flattened into a sponging apparatus. Its feet, too, are different. Instead of claws, there are pads which secrete a sticky substance, enabling the fly to walk on walls and ceilings. This arrangement also enables house flies to spread disease, because the bacteria on their feet will be deposited with the secretion.

The biting fly that often enters our houses before storms is the stable fly, very similar in appearance to the house fly, but with biting mouthparts.

In warm weather, it takes only two weeks for a generation of house flies to be produced. Eggs hatch in twenty-four hours, and maggots are ready to pupate in five days. When you see a small fly, don't be misled into thinking it is a young fly still growing. With flies, as with all insects, once the winged stage has been reached, there is no further growth. There simply are small flies and large ones, just as there are small dogs and large ones. As a matter of fact,

Enormous compound eyes dominate the head of the horse fly. With them flies detect motion from any direction. Added to their agile flying ability, this keen eyesight makes them difficult to capture.

The horse fly's compound eyes are striped with brilliant bands of color. In the eye each lens is a hexagon.

Seen at close range, house flies are surprisingly hairy. A sticky substance on their feet enables them to walk on walls and ceilings. Their feet spread disease by picking up and depositing bacteria.

Slender-bodied and humpbacked, this robber fly is a voracious assassin. It seizes other insects in mid-air, then carries them to a perch where it sucks the carcass dry. Notice the haltere — the white knob on the thorax.

This furry masquerader is not a bumblebee. It is actually a robber fly, hoping to frighten away enemies with its deceptive pose. Its two wings mark it clearly as a fly; bees have four wings.

flies comprise one of the largest insect orders. There are sixteen thousand species in the United States—twice the number of kinds of moths and butterflies.

Gall Flies   Some insects, with the aid of certain chemicals, are able to induce plants to build homes for them, providing both protection and food. These overgrown areas of plant tissue are known as galls. They seem to be the plant equivalent of tumors in man or animals. Because of this rapid increase in cell growth and reproduction scientists are very interested in them. They may give clues to how cancers develop. Each kind of gall insect—and besides flies these may be midges, wasps, or aphids—produces a gall of a particular shape and texture

Besides being an excellent place to hunt for insects, a field of goldenrod is host to myriads of gall-forming flies.

Many goldenrod stems have a rounded swelling, or gall, caused by the larva of a small fly. This overgrowth of stem tissue provides food and shelter for the developing fly larva.

The gall itself becomes hard and tan, about the size of a walnut. Similar to tumors in animals, these tissue growths are studied by scientists who hope to learn more about cancer.

on a particular kind of plant. Some plants are host to many gall insects. Three hundred kinds infest oaks. Goldenrod, roses, and willows are hosts to many others.

When you walk through a field of goldenrod, look carefully at the stems. More than half the plants in the field will have a rounded swelling on the stem —a gall caused by a very small fly with spotted, or "pictured," wings. In early summer, the female lays an egg on the stem. The larva hatches, wanders a bit, then burrows into the stem and begins to eat. The feeding activity of the larva stimulates the plant to produce extra tissue in that area, which eventually becomes the size of a walnut. By fall the larva stops eating, chews a tunnel almost to the outside of the gall, leaving a thin layer, and then pupates. When the adult fly emerges in spring it has no means of chewing but is able to leave the gall simply by pushing its way out head first through the thin layer of remaining gall skin. If you find a gall with a tiny hole in it you know that the mature fly has already exited. If there is no hole, the small cream-colored maggot is still inside.

84

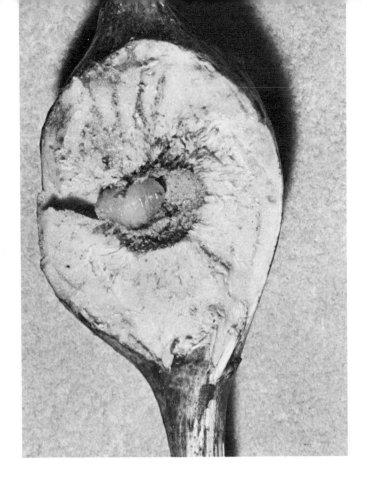

The cream-colored larva eats the tissues inside the gall and gnaws a tunnel for when it is ready to leave. After the pupa state it will have no jaws.

Legless, soft-bodied, and very small, the larva pupates inside the gall. The adult fly exits through the previously gnawed hole.

flies that are not flies

Every insect with wings is not a fly, just as every insect that crawls is not a bug. For centuries people have been misnaming animals after only a quick glance. But when scientists began sorting creatures sytematically, they looked closer and realized that superficial appearance could be misleading. What they looked for was more fundamental structural similarities.

True flies of course have only two wings, with the hind pair replaced by the balancers, the halteres. All insects with four wings belong to other orders, though many may be called flies.

Caddisflies   As a larva living in a pond or stream, a young caddisfly builds a kind of tubular house to protect its soft, caterpillar-shaped body. It hauls this house around wherever it goes, anchoring itself firmly to the bottom of the tube by hooks at the end of the body. In times of danger it withdraws its dark head and thorax inside. When all's clear, it sticks out its head and legs again, and walks along underwater, dragging the case behind. The foundation of the house is silk, and, varying with the kind of caddisworm, it is reinforced by bits of sand, wood splinters, very small pebbles, or pieces of plant stem which are glued to the foundation with a sticky mouth secretion. Some cases look like animated log cabins, some like part of a miniature stone wall. As the larva grows, more material is added to the open front end of the tube. Quiet ponds are populated by caddisworms that may build a tube of sand, each grain carefully chosen to fit its neighbors, or by larvae that snip bits of plant tissue, sometimes still green, and lay them lengthwise along the silk tube. Stream caddisworms, on the other hand, build turtle-shaped mounds of pebbles half an inch long. They glue their houses to rocks to keep them from being washed away in the current. Another kind of caddisworm spins a net of silk to trap the microscopic forms of life it eats. Yet in spite of these elaborate shields, caddisworms are eaten in great numbers. Half a brook trout's diet is caddisworms.

It takes about a year for caddisflies to develop. Eggs laid one summer become adults the next. They winter in the larval stage. To pupate, the larva spins a cocoon inside the case. This pupa is more active than most, for when the adult is ready to emerge, the pupa cuts the silk cocoon, swims to the surface, and crawls out. Then the skin splits a final time to reveal the adult, which looks like a slender dusky moth with long wings and long threadlike antennae. Adult caddisflies are inactive by day, but are attracted to lights at night. Most adults have no functional mouthparts, and do not eat. Fishermen call the adults "duns," and make dry flies to imitate them. Wet fly models are also popular, shaped like the larvae that are so attractive to fish.

Mayflies
It may take a mayfly nymph three years to develop into an adult that lives for only a few hours. Mayflies belong to the order Ephemerida, which aptly means "living for a short time." During its underwater life in a pond or brook, the nymph may molt twenty times. It is very active, clambering about under stones or swimming gracefully in search of plant food. Seven pairs of external gills extract oxygen from the water and give the abdomen a feathered appearance. Enemies are legion — mayflies are a succulent part of the diet of many fish, salamanders, turtles, dragonfly nymphs and other aquatic insects.

When mayflies are ready to become adults, they climb out of the water, molt again, and the winged adult is soon ready to fly. But this adult goes a step farther. It actually molts again after it has wings. It is the only insect that does this. The molt may occur in flight, within minutes or hours after it becomes airborne. In the interim, the reproductive organs will have matured. In their final form, the delicate shining wings are held vertically over the back, while two or three long harmless filaments trail from the end of the abdomen.

Adults have no mouthparts and hence never eat. Their brief lives are just long enough for them to mate in flight and drop eggs into the water. The adults emerge from the water in swarms, and often heaps of windblown bodies are found on lake shores. They are attracted to lights, and may be eaten by bats, toads and nocturnal birds. Both as young and adults they make fine fish lures. Adult mayfly models have been given poetic names, like "the silver gray" and "the evening spinner."

Stoneflies
Stonefly nymphs are important fish food too, but they prefer to live in swift water. Their gills are not as efficient as mayflies', so they must live in well-aerated water. Flattened and black, the nymphs seek dark places, scuttling with a sidling gait when a stone is lifted. They too have many enemies. Some mature early in the year and run about over the snow in January and February. The blunt-headed adults are weak flyers and often hide under leaves. One female may lay six thousand eggs, attesting to the hazardous life of the immature forms. Adults live brief lives, eating little or nothing.

Dobsonfly
Bright lights may also attract the dramatically large dobsonfly. It can be two inches long, with mottled wings and curved mandibles that look like dangerous calipers. Males have a much longer pair — half as long as the body — but they

Wherever the caddisworm goes, it drags along its portable house. This tubular structure protects the larva from underwater dangers its soft body would otherwise be exposed to. When frightened, it draws its head and thorax inside, out of sight.

Like the dragonfly, the caddisfly grows up underwater, but lives in the air as an adult. But unlike the dragonfly, this mothlike insect never eats.

are used only to hold the female during mating. The female's shorter mandibles are much more likely to pinch hard.

These insects develop in streams. The larvae are carnivorous, preying on other water insects and growing to a squirmy three-inch-length with thick tough skin. After three years of being fiercely predatory, they are ready to pupate. They crawl out of the river to find a suitable place under a stone or moss on the bank. Long a favorite fish bait, the larva has many names: hellgramite, conniption-bug, crawler, hell-devil. The eggs from which they hatch are laid, two to three thousand at a time, in a white waxy inch-wide mat on a leaf overhanging a stream.

Golden-Eyed Lacewing Fly Gauzy, pale green wings give the adult lacewing a graceful fairylike look, but the young are ugly and are particularly fond of aphids. About once a minute, the larva impales an aphid on its scimitarlike mandibles. Exuding a fluid that predigests the insect, the larva then sucks the liquid food through the hollow jaws. The empty aphid skin is tossed aside and the larva attacks the next aphid. Incredibly hungry, these spiny triangular larvae with tapering abdomens can almost keep up with the superfast reproductive rate of aphids. When it is ready to pupate, the larva spins a round silk cocoon a quarter inch in diameter under a leaf and pupates inside. When it is time to emerge, the pupa slices the silk almost all the way around the top, leaving a silken hinge. Then the adult climbs out and expands its four delicate cross-veined wings.

Adults, too, eat aphids. Lacewings in fact are a boon in the garden, but you may not even suspect their presence until dusk, when winds die down, and the weak-flying adults come to a porch light. Their eyes glitter gold and are iridescent in the light. If you happen to touch this beauty, you may notice an unpleasant odor on your hands. This comes from secretions of the insect's thoracic glands—a protective device that gives lacewings another name—stinkflies. If you do capture a female and put her into a jar along with a plant stalk (preferably colonized by aphids), you may get a chance to watch her egg-laying process. The female performs like a skilled glassblower, secreting a pool of silk on a leaf, and then raising the tip of her abdomen, bringing with it a stalk of stiff silk which hardens in the air as she works. On top of this quarter-inch stem she deposits an egg. She then builds another stalk for the second egg—almost as if she knew how gluttonous her young would be when they

After several years as a nymph underwater, the adult mayfly lives only a few hours in the air. But its brief life is uniquely active. It is the only insect that sheds its skin after having grown wings. After molting, it mates, lays its eggs, and dies. Like the caddisfly, it does not eat.

The stonefly nymph lives in swift streams because it needs bubbly water to breathe. The blunt-headed adult appears as early as February, even when there is snow on the ground. A poor flyer, it often hides under leaves.

hatch. Even with the stalks, some cannibalism takes place. But if the female has been careful in her choice of egg-laying site, the larvae will attack aphid after aphid instead of each other.

Ant Lion   Another voracious larva actually builds a trap to snare its food. In sandy areas where there is a overhang to keep out rain, the ant lion digs a cone-shaped pit by flicking many loads of sand out with the back of its head. Then it lies in wait at the bottom, completely buried except for its curved mandibles and the top of its head. When an ant or another small walker blunders into the steep-sided cone, an avalanche begins, abetted by the efforts of the buried ant lion, who keeps flicking sand to make the footing more treacherous. When the prey is within reach, the ant lion seizes it, injects a digestive fluid and sucks its meal, then tosses the empty carcass out of the pit. This kind of passive trapping depends on how many insects of suitable size wander by, so the larval life-span varies. It is usually about two years. But finally it pupates, also in the sand, and so cleverly does it spin that there is never any sand inside the

No larger than the eye of a needle, lacewing eggs are protectively isolated at the top of quarter-inch stalks. The cannibalistic larvae, which hatch simultaneously, would eat their brothers and sisters if they could get to them.

Special mandibles enable the lacewing pupa to slice a neat exit in its silken cocoon. After emerging, it molts and becomes an adult.

cocoon, even though it is completely surrounded by sand. When the adult emerges, it spreads its four long tapering net-veined wings to dry. Its activities now will be to find a mate and (for the female) to lay eggs. Then it will perish. Strangely enough, the adult has no common name: it is simply known as an adult ant lion.

Four gauzy wings and brilliant golden eyes give the adult lacewing a striking appearance. A poor flyer, it is seen most often at dusk and at other times when the wind is low.

beetles

If people varied in size as much as beetles do, the tallest adult would be four hundred times as big as the shortest instead of merely twice. Of all the insect groups, beetles have the greatest range in size. The smallest is only one hundredth of an inch long—so small it can easily crawl through the eye of a needle. The largest, the Goliath beetle of Africa, is the size of a mouse—about four inches long. Between these extremes there are 250,000 other species of beetles in the world, 23,000 of them United States residents. This is more than three times the number of local moths and butterflies and makes beetles the most varied of all groups of insects in both the U.S.A. and the world.

Diets in the beetle world range as widely as size. Live-meat-eaters climb trees to hunt for caterpillars or dig tunnels in the ground to wait unseen, ready to seize ambulatory food. Some make inroads in the snail and slug population; others prefer aphid colonies. A dead mouse is very attractive to scavenging beetles. Some kinds bury it and feed on the meat. Others eat the tougher skin and sinew. Beetles chew the leaves of plants, eat flowers, bore stems, munch roots, seeds, and pollen. Some even eat wood. The drugstore beetle has the strangest diet of all—it can live on a steady diet of red pepper.

All beetles, regardless of size or appetite, are easily recognized by their thickened veinless front wings which meet in a straight line down the middle of the back and cover their transparent hind wings. All have strong chewing jaws enabling them to attack their food efficiently. Many kinds live in the ground, some run about on it, some tunnel under the bark of trees, while others live in ponds and streams. Beetle larvae, called grubs, often live in quite different ways from the adults.

Predators The tiger beetle, as vividly colored and fierce as its namesake, is a night hunter, running rapidly over the ground or climbing trees in quest of caterpillars. The larva is known as a doodlebug, and it is just as bloodthirsty as the adult. Its method of hunting is different, however. Instead of climbing it hides in a vertical burrow in the ground. When another insect walks by, it reaches out to seize and eat it.

One ground beetle, the "fiery searcher," has an unusual appetite for hairy food, seeking out insects like tent caterpillars or gypsy moth larvae. It climbs trees at night to hunt them. Like many of its relatives, it can produce a blistering fluid to defend itself.

Fireflies, in spite of their name, are actually beetles. Their wing covers are softer than most beetles', but they do have two pairs of wings instead of a fly's single pair. Firefly light is a form of "cold light" the insects produce chemically. They need extra oxygen to do this and thus are likely to die sooner than other insects if confined in a jar. They are luminous in all stages of their lives. The larva glows even before it hatches from the egg. Once hatched, these "glow worms" can easily be spotted by their flashes in swampy areas on warm spring evenings. In these wet places they find the snails and slugs which make up

Like turtles, beetles are shielded from danger by their heavy exoskeletons. This shell, dull orange with black spots, is an inch long.

A bright orange dome with black spots quickly identifies the ladybug. And the shell-like front wings show that it is a member of the beetle family. Here, a ladybug attacks a favorite item on its menu — an aphid.

Similar in color and eating habits to the adult, the black-and-orange ladybug larva also eats large quantities of aphids. The mother lays her eggs near aphid colonies, so the hatching larvae will have a ready supply of food.

The last skin shed by the ladybug larva can be seen below this pupa. While it hangs upside down, the larva inside changes into its adult form.

This brown beetle with yellow stripes is the adult rustic borer. Its larvae eat tunnels in evergreen trees and live on a diet of wood.

their diet. Adults eat little or nothing. They use their light to signal for a mate. Each species of firefly has its own individual pattern of flashes.

Dome-shaped ladybugs are another kind of beetle. They advertise their unpalatability to enemies by their bright colors. Depending on the species, a single ladybug may have up to nineteen black spots. Both the hairy, black and orange checkered larvae and the glistening orange adults live exclusively on aphids and their noxious relatives, such as mealy bugs and scale insects, wolfing quantitites of them. Eggs are laid near aphid colonies, and the newly hatched larvae get right to work. When they are ready to pupate, they glue the hind end of their body to a leaf, hang upside down, and transform in this position. The adults hibernate, often in clusters.

Adult blister beetles are vegetarians, but not the larvae. Some larvae are equipped with sticky pads. They wait on flowers until a bee comes by, then hitchhike to the hive where they eat bee eggs. Another larva feeds on buried pods of grasshopper eggs, thus reducing the number of eggs that hatch.

Scavengers Adult carrion beetles, equipped with digging claws, can bury a dead mouse or a small bird in a few hours simply by undermining it. The eggs which are laid on the carcass hatch quickly, and the larvae have such a plentiful supply of meat that they may become adults in a week.

When there is nothing but skin and sinew left, other scavenging beetles take over. They are so thorough about cleaning up a skeleton that scientists use them for removing bits of tissue from delicate skeletons.

A magnified view of the rustic borer. The sensory hairs on this beetle's body help it feel what is going on around it. These hairs are particularly useful where its skeleton is thick.

A relative of these scavengers is the hairy carpet beetle, the household pest who lives on woolen carpets. Again, the larva is the hungry stage.

Scarab beetles—members of a large family—have been symbols of immortality since Egyptian times. The reason for this may be that a few scarab beetles would be seen entering the ground while many would emerge a short time later. A number of scarab beetles are brightly colored. All have polished wing covers and long spiny legs. Their antennae are distinctive, too, the tips being made of broadened plates which can be spread wide or folded tightly. Scavenging scarab beetles live on dung which they bury. In some species, pairs of beetles roll dung into balls, a habit which gives them the name "tumblebugs."

The milkweed beetle is bright orange with black spots. The wings you see — the fore wings, which meet in a straight line down the middle of its back—are not used for flying. The beetle flies with its lighter hind wings, which are folded underneath the front pair.

Gardeners are well acquainted with this voracious vegetarian—the Japanese beetle. It lives on a variety of flowers, leaves, and fruit, and can be recognized by its forked antennae and long, spiny legs.

Vegetarians June bugs should really be called May beetles, for it is on warm nights in May that we begin to hear them bumbling and bumping on our screens. So heavy-bodied are these bronze beetles that they must pump up internal sacs with air before they can take off. They are strongly attracted to light. Dozens can be found scattered over the screens of a porch if the light is left on for even half an hour. They are scarabs along with the rose chafer and the Japanese beetle, two other vegetarian cousins, and all of them can be recognized by their unusual antennae and long spiny legs. The white, C-shaped grubs of all three beetles feed on grass roots. They are often present in large enough numbers to damage lawns and golf courses.

May beetle adults eat tree leaves, adult rose chafers (who appear in June) live on flower leaves and petals, while bronzy-green Japanese beetles (who mature in July) eat a variety of leaves, flowers, and fruit. These destructive green beetles were accidentally introduced in New Jersey from the Orient in 1916, and since then they have flourished and spread over much of the country.

Children delight in finding a narrow-bodied click beetle, for each time it is turned on its back, it leaps into the air with an audible click in an effort to right itself. To do this, the insect arches its body to remove a prong from a groove on the thorax, then suddenly snaps the prong back in place with enough force to send the insect upward a foot. It may land on its back again, but needs only repeat the process to right itself. The larva is a tan, hard-skinned, long, slender grub known as a wireworm. Because these larvae feed on the roots of plants, they are serious crop pests. There can be as many as 200,000 of them in an acre of soil.

Legions of leaf beetles, many with gaudy stripes or spots, are economic problems, too. They devour leaves of crop and garden plants to the tune of millions of dollars every year. Because these beetles specialize, and because crops are planted with row after row of identical plants, the leaf beetles lead an ideal existence, never having to wonder where their next meal is coming from. They simply move down the line. The Colorado potato beetle, the asparagus beetle, and the cucumber beetle are members of this large family.

The golden tortoise beetle is the "goldbug" Edgar Allan Poe immortalized in his short story. It has transparent margins around its body, leaving a dark area in the center shaped like a turtle. Its favorite leaves belong to plants in the morning glory family. Its nickname comes from its unique ability to change color from dull brick to shining gold. But a dead goldbug is always dull red-brown, to the dismay of collectors.

When you pick up an acorn with a hole in it, you probably have in your hand the former home of a young weevil. If you collect acorns in the fall, you may later find that a collection of "worms" has emerged from the acorns to pupate. These weevil grubs are small, light-colored, and curved. Some relatives destroy stored beans or peas. Others, like the cotton boll weevil, are notorious for the amount of crop damage they do.

Wood Borers People cannot digest cellulose in any form, but many kinds of beetles manage to live on a steady diet of wood cellulose. Those that bore in solid wood need two or three years to mature, but this period may be stretched to fifteen or twenty years if the wood is cut and built into furniture or used for beams. It is strange but possible to have adult beetles emerge from the chair you're sitting in. Flooring, too, may be peppered with small holes and beams may be hollowed to mere shells by such wood eaters.

When bark is removed from a dead tree, the channels of the wood-boring beetles show up. The pattern and width of these tunnels are distinctive for each kind of beetle. One type is meandering, broad, and flat. Another looks like a sunburst pattern, for the mother engraver beetle chews a straight tunnel under the bark, with regular rows of short side chambers, in each of which she lays an egg. When the grubs hatch, they each gnaw outward, making larger tunnels as they increase in size. The whole brood creates a fan of tunnels on each side of the primary tunnel. A relative, the elm bark beetle, lives under

This black-and-yellow locust borer sips nectar from a field of goldenrod. Though it has no sting, its wasplike appearance protects it from birds and other attackers.

The woolly weevil uses its sharp proboscis to bore holes in acorns and other hard seeds. Eggs laid in these holes produce grubs, which eat the starch in the seeds.

the bark and is responsible for spreading the fungus that causes Dutch elm disease.

Several wood borers can make noises. The death watch beetles bang their bodies against the walls of their galleries and this small noise can be heard at night when it is quiet. Shiny black "bessybugs" make a grating noise by rubbing abdomen against wing covers.

Water Beetles   Whirligig beetles gyrate in dizzy circles on the surface of ponds or slow-moving streams. If they are alarmed, they dive, but they must return to the surface for air for all water beetles are air breathers. When they dive, whirligigs carry a bubble of air at the tip of the abdomen. These beetles are shaped like watermelon seeds and are just as hard to hold, for they are slippery and active. They appear to have two compound eyes on each side of the head, but it is really one, divided on the outside by a bridge of tissue. The upper half of the eye scans the air, while the lower half looks into the water. When handled, whirligigs give off a milky fluid that smells like apples to most people. They are scavengers, feeding on the bodies of insects that fall into the water.

The diving beetle is an active hunter. With its strong jaws it is big enough

Extending from the middle of the weevil's proboscis are two elbowed antennae. When the proboscis is in use, the antennae fold back into grooves.

Dead trees, stripped of their bark, reveal the broad tunnels of boring beetle larvae. The grooves become wider as the larvae grow.

to devour small tadpoles, tiny fish, and insects. It is an inch long, dark, flat, and edged with brown. Its hind legs are fringed and oarlike. It is often seen hanging head down from the surface, collecting under its fore wings a supply of air to use below. The larva is properly called a water tiger, for it has dangerous-looking, curved mandibles and an appetite to match. But it has a different method of eating from the adult. Its prey—any aquatic creature of reasonable size—is injected with a liquid which digests the meat before it is sucked through a groove on the mandible. Adults may live several years, hibernating under water with an occasional active period. Sometimes they can be seen through clear ice, swimming about as though it were summer. Air pockets trapped under the ice furnish them with oxygen when the pond is sealed off from the air above.

Other wood-beetle larvae form sunburst patterns with their tunnels under the bark. The mother laid her eggs in the straight tunnels; the young grubs ate their way outward in haphazard paths.

The diving beetle is well adapted to underwater life. Fringes on its hind legs make them effective oars.

Although it lives underwater, the inch-long diving beetle has no gills. To get air it hangs head downward from the surface and fills a storage area under its wings. Then it returns to stalking tadpoles and small fish.

stingers

Real stinging equipment has been developed by only one group of insects: the order Hymenoptera, meaning "membrane wings." This order includes the ants, wasps, and bees. But not all Hymenoptera have the ability. There are stingless bees as well as stingless ants. And no male of any species can sting. For a stinger is, in fact, a modified ovipositor, a sharp probe at the end of the female's abdomen, with venom glands to discharge poison through it. In most cases this elaborate apparatus is used primarily to paralyze food for the young rather than for defense.

Two kinds of social wasps, yellow jackets and bald-faced hornets, are the most generous with their stings, though to be fair, they are only likely to be vicious when their nests are disturbed or approached too closely. Their venom is potent, and they are able to sting repeatedly since their stingers are unbarbed. These wasps are banded with black and yellow and can be distinguished from flies with similar color patterns by their four transparent wings, as against the flies' two.

When a bee or wasp stings a person, the reaction to the venom may be violent if his body has become sensitized to the injected proteins. A sensitized person is allergic to the venom and each additional sting may cause shock or even death. Persons who develop increasingly severe reactions have two courses open to them: they can either have a series of "shots" to immunize them against the venom or they can carry medication to be taken immediately if they should be stung.

Social Wasps Wasps were making paper thousands of years before the Chinese discovered the art. Any sort of weathered wood is acceptable raw material—a fence, a building, or even a lawn chair. The wasp rasps off shreds of wood with its strong mandibles, making a barely audible sound. On the way back to the nest, the wood pulp is chewed thoroughly and mixed with saliva. Upon reaching the nest, it is spread into a thin layer to dry. The source of wood fibers may vary in color, producing a banded effect on the nest.

Each football-shaped nest of the bald-faced hornet is built during one summer and is vacant by fall. The thousands of wasp citizens in one paper city succumb to the cold; only the fertile queen hibernates, in a protected place such as under tree bark or in an attic, while last summer's nest is battered by winter storms. When the temperature rises again in the spring, the queen constructs a hemisphere of paper. Inside this she builds a small horizontal comb of paper cells and lays an egg in each. She raises the first brood of workers alone—no simple task—for she must build and hunt as well as feed the larvae. No food is stored in the nest. She lives on nectar, but she catches insects (mostly flies) and chops them up to feed the young. The full grown larvae spin silk caps over their cells just before they pupate.

When this first brood is mature, they take over the chores and the queen

The bald-faced hornet has a vicious temper if its nest is threatened. Here, its sideways-moving jaws rasp fibers from a dead stump of wood. With this wood the hornet will make paper to construct its large, football-shaped nest.

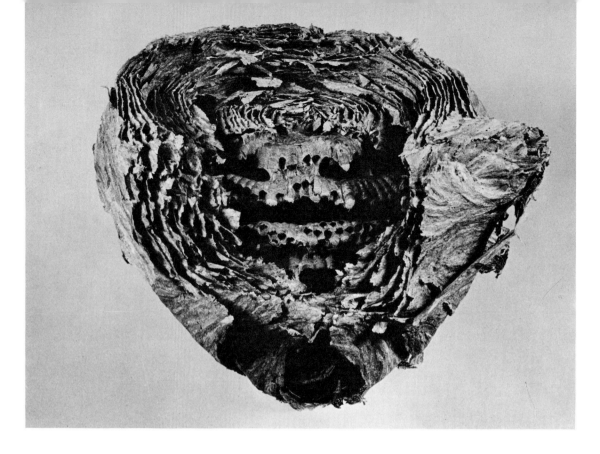

A cross-sectional view reveals how many layers of paper, with air spaces in between, insulate the hornet's nest. The location of the entrance, at the bottom, helps keep rain out.

At the core of the hornet's nest are the horizontal combs, shown on the right. Both the cells and the nest walls are made of paper. Each cell layer hangs from the one above by a strong stem.

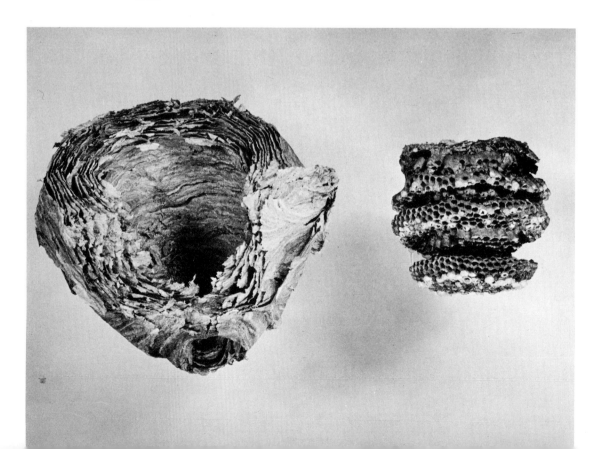

can then concentrate on egg-laying. The more workers there are, the faster the nest grows. New layers of brood cells are added, each suspended by a strong stem from the one above. The envelopes of paper are enlarged as the nest grows. These thin layers of paper, with the air spaces between, are very effective as insulation; they help to keep the nest at an even temperature. If the nest gets too hot, the wasps cool it by evaporation: they bring water to the nest, wet the paper, then fan it with their thin wings. The entrance to the city is always at the bottom, protected from rain. In a large nest, this is an active area, for workers are constantly returning from expeditions in search of building materials or baby food.

Yellow jackets are smaller than bald-faced hornets, but appear to have much sharper tempers. They build their paper nests underground. The larger European hornets choose hollow trees and build coarser nests. A mild-mannered cousin, the brown Polistes, builds a small open nest under eaves of buildings. Seldom do more than a dozen wasps occupy this nest, which has no enclosing envelopes. These wasps are said to chirp as they work.

Solitary Wasps Not all wasps live in colonies, nor do they all make paper. Some use mud mixed with saliva which forms, when dry, a much more durable material than mud alone. The thread-waisted potter wasp makes jugs of mud on shrubs; another

The brown Polistes wasp builds its nest under the eaves of buildings. Unlike the hornet, the queen does not cover the outside with paper walls. In the open cells, her young can be seen in many stages of growing up.

The adult Polistes sucks nectar from such flowers as the goldenrod, above. The young, on the other hand, eat insects, which the mother catches and carries back to them in the nest.

Not all wasps build their homes of paper. Some use mud, arranged in a herringbone pattern like this. Inside, the mother lays her eggs on an insect which she has paralyzed with her sting and carried back to the nest. The larvae live as parasites on this insect.

wasp builds tubes of mud against a wall in a geometric herringbone pattern, while the steel-blue mud dauber pastes her cells over with dabs of mud. This nest is no architectural beauty, but it may be decorative because each mouthful of mud is a different color. All these mud cells are stocked with spiders or insects intended as food for the larvae. The mother wasp stings the prey carefully, enough to paralyze but not kill, then lays an egg on it. The grub then has fresh food available.

If you should find a slanting burrow in the ground on a hard-packed path through the woods or in a sand bank, it's well worth watching. It may be the nest of a digger wasp, and you may be able to watch the last stage of excavation. Then the female will fly around the site in ever widening circles to get her bearings before going off in search of an insect. When she returns, she will take her carefully paralyzed prize down into the burrow where she lays an egg on it. Some digger wasps have been known to use a pebble to tamp the opening after the cell has been loaded; others leave the burrow open and bring fresh food as the growing larva requires it. The largest of the digger wasps is called the cicada-killer; it favors these musical insects as baby food. The burrow is large—the diameter of a pencil—and is often dug in lawns. In spite of its large size, a cicada-killer is not nearly as dangerous as its gregarious cousins, for none of the solitary wasps stings readily. They use their stingers chiefly for paralyzing food for their young.

Many plant galls, particularly on oaks, are caused by small wasps, which as larvae eat the walls of their homes. The overgrown areas of plant tissue form as a result of these invasions.

Ichneumon wasps (erroneously called flies) are among the most frightening-looking insects because of their enormously long ovipositors—sometimes four inches long. The long trailing filaments are not used for stinging, however, but as accessory tools for drilling into trees in order to lay an egg on the larva of another insect already there. Ichneumon wasps are beneficial since

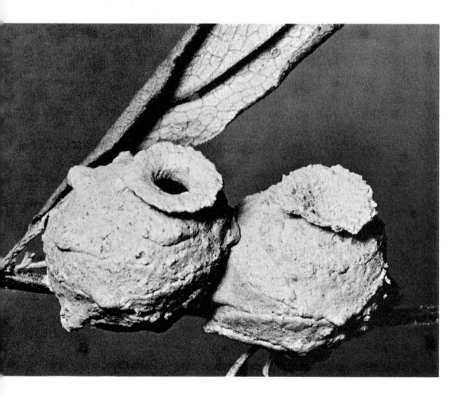

The potter wasp balances its nests, mouth upward, on shrub twigs. The openings are plugged after the eggs are laid. Inside these mud houses, the larvae live on paralyzed caterpillars or beetle grubs.

they destroy boring insects that cause so much damage. No one yet knows how the wasps are able to tell where to drill.

Solitary Bees   Some time or other you may have noticed circular pieces missing from wild rose leaves. This is the nesting material of a solitary bee. It makes a burrow inside a woody plant stem, dividing it up into cells by making walls of rose leaves. Each cell contains an egg, and food in the form of a pollen and nectar mixture for the developing bee.

Black carpenter bees sometimes choose beams to mine as a nesting site, and can do much damage before they are discovered.

Social Bees   Honeybees are not native to the United States. They were brought by early colonists. The Indians called them the "white man's fly." Wild honeybees now are descendants of swarms that escaped from apiaries and have reverted to their ancient habit of nesting in hollow trees. Although honeybees are sometimes considered domesticated, it is man who has learned to adjust to the bees' habits, and to glean honey and wax. The bees themselves have simply continued to live their complicated lives, and manage quite well should they become "wild."

Honeybees have methodical habits that turn out to be useful to man. When a bee is gathering pollen, it visits flower after flower of the same kind. Pollen grains adhere easily to the branched hairs on the bee's body, and from time to time they are combed out of the "fur" and packed into a hollow on the hind leg called the pollen basket. Pollen is thus carried from flower to flower, making possible a high level of seed production. Without the aid of insects— especially bees—orchards would produce little fruit.

Bees are confirmed vegetarians. They eat nothing but plant products. Pollen gives them fat and protein, while nectar provides carbohydrates. A mixture of the two, beebread, is the major food of the larvae. Foraging bees collect either nectar or pollen on any one trip, never both. Nectar, a dilute sugar water, is carried home by bees in a special honey crop, where chemicals change it from a complex to a simple sugar. After it is stored in the hive for a while, enough water will have evaporated to make it very thick; only then is it honey.

One of the most interesting discoveries of recent years is that bees have a language. A field bee can communicate the direction and distance of a rich source of food by dancing on the comb, and giving a sample of what is to be collected.

Each honeybee has a special job to do depending on its age. New workers are housekeepers. They clean the brood cells and keep the developing bees warm. When the workers are three days old, they graduate to feeding the older grubs, each of which gets many beebread meals a day. By the time workers are six days old, special feeding glands develop that secrete a substance rich in B vitamins. This is called royal jelly. All larvae receive this mixture for their first few days, and then their diet is changed to beebread for the rest of their larval lives. But a larva that will become a queen is fed only royal jelly for the entire grub stage. Diet apparently is a significant factor in determining whether a larva becomes a worker or a queen.

A two-week-old worker has reached the stage of its life when feeding glands subside and wax glands develop. Very small plates of wax are exuded from the underside of the abdomen. They are chewed and used for building cells. About four days later the wax glands become inactive and the worker becomes a guard, whose job it is to keep out any bee that does not have the particular hive odor. Defending the hive may mean suicide, for a honeybee's stinger is barbed and cannot be withdrawn without tearing the bee's body apart. At the age of three weeks, workers become field bees, foraging widely for nectar and pollen. So strenuous is this life that a field bee is often worn and tattered by the time it is six weeks old. One pound of honey represents sixty thousand trips of about a mile and a half each. Wax making is even more expensive in terms of energy, for a pound of wax requires the consumption of six pounds of honey.

A hive is home to about fifteen thousand bees, all descendants of the same mother. Most of these bees are workers (females, since they have ovipositors, but undeveloped, since they cannot lay eggs). A few are males, "drones." There is only one queen, and she does nothing but lay eggs, so there is a continuous succession of bees of all ages. Workers develop from fertilized eggs, but the stingless drones, whose only function is to mate with new queens, develop from unfertilized eggs. When the hive becomes too crowded, the old queen leaves the hive with half the workers. This swarm will find a new place to live. While the scouts from the swarm are searching for a suitable site, the bees form a hanging cluster in a convenient place; they are not dangerous at this time, since they all gorged on honey before they left the old hive. The old queen leaves just before special queen cells, peanut-shaped and much larger than brood cells, produce new queens who will battle until only one remains. The victor then flies to mate in the air, and then returns to the hive to lay eggs for the rest of her life. The drones, having fulfilled their purpose, are driven out of the hive in the fall. The honey they would have eaten becomes part of the hive's winter store of food.

Bumblebees   In contrast to the honeybee, the big furry bumblebees do not survive the winter as colonies, nor do they store food. Only the queen hibernates. In early spring, she cruises about, hunting for an abandoned mousehole in which she can set up housekeeping. She makes a honeypot of wax and builds a few cells in which to lay eggs. Like the queen bald-faced hornet, she raises the first brood

The larvae of these wasps, known as sawflies, devour large quantities of evergreen needles.
Feeding in groups, they can be very destructive to ornamental shrubs.

herself, doing all the necessary foraging, building, and feeding. When the first workers mature, they take over these tasks, and she stays at home laying eggs.

Unlike the honeybee, bumblebees gather both pollen and nectar on any one trip. These bees are natives, and have very long tongues suitable for reaching nectaries deep in tubular flowers. Red clover has flowers like this, and only bumblebees are equipped to collect nectar from them and in the process, cross-

Under the curled petal of a wild sunflower, a solitary bee finds shelter for the night.

Three bees at work in their nest. They can be identified as workers because of their size (the queen is much larger) and because they are working — something the drones never do. The workers perform a variety of tasks — keep house, feed the grubs and queen, and forage for nectar and pollen.

pollinate them. When red clover fields were planted in Australia, there were few seeds produced until bumblebees were imported.

The bumblebee's stinger is smooth and so she is able to sting repeatedly without sacrificing her life in defense of the hive. Mice—competitors for nesting sites—are stung much more often than human beings are.

An attentive circle of workers clean and feed the larger queen honeybee (center). Her only function is to lay eggs.

ant or termite?

A worldwide insect census would show that there are more individual ants than any other kind of insect. It would also show that not a single ant lives alone. Each ant is specialized for a particular role in an ant society. The social colony survives as a whole, with each type of ant contributing a function that is impossible for the others.

A distinctive hourglass body shape makes any ant easy to recognize, whether it's brown, black, red, or yellow; whether it's a fifteenth of an inch or a whole inch long. At the top of the head is a pair of elbow-shaped antennae, which are very sensitive to odors and touch. Lower down are the jaws, which are used primarily as hands. The legs are strong and attached to the thorax, as are the temporary wings of the reproductive forms. The thorax itself is separated from the abdomen by a very narrow waist—the easiest way to distinguish ants from broad-bodied termites. Some kinds of ants have well-developed stingers at the end of the abdomen, like wasps and bees, but other kinds bite first and then squirt poison into the wound from the tip of the abdomen.

Most of the ants in a nest are workers. These are wingless, infertile females. Soldier ants are also infertile females but with larger heads and jaws. The queen is the only egg producer in the colony. The workers care for her and feed her, enlarge the nest, gather food, and care for the developing eggs, larvae, and pupae. At intervals, groups of the pupae become winged males and females, which swarm in large numbers. One of the most astonishing things about ants is the fact that nests of the same species in a large area produce such swarms simultaneously, thus increasing the possibility of cross-fertilization. No one knows what the signal is that sets them off or how they could possibly communicate their plans.

Males live only brief lives, dying soon after the nuptial flight. The newly mated queen, however, will live for ten or fifteen years. Ready to start her new colony, her first act is to press her wings against plant stems, breaking them off along a pre-weakened line just above their bases. Then she burrows into the soil in a suitable spot and lays her first eggs. During the next few months she gathers no food, but lives on energy from dissolving wing muscles. She also eats a number of the eggs she lays. The first group of workers she raises

To tell an ant from a termite, look at the shape of the body: the ant has a pinpoint waist between its thorax and abdomen; the termite's body is broad, narrowing only slightly between head and thorax. The wings have not yet developed on these termite nymphs.

is small because of the limited food supply, but once mature, they take over the chores of excavation, food gathering and hunting, and feeding of the young. Tunnels are dug, and chambers for eggs, larvae, and pupae are enlarged. (Ant eggs are not laid in separate cells in the way of bees and wasps, but are piled into underground rooms. The young are moved toward the surface or deeper into the ground depending on temperature and moisture.)

Ant larvae are white, curved, and legless, with a body tapering toward the head. They are fed partly digested food regurgitated by the workers, who in turn obtain some of their nourishment from a glandular secretion of the larvae. This mutual food exchange is one strong bond that keeps ants colonial.

Pupae sometimes spin a thin papery cocoon, sometimes not, depending

The winged queen ant swarms into the air with the males and other queens. After mating, she drops to the ground, breaks off her wings, and starts her colony. Her only task then is to lay eggs.

Scattered sawdust indicates the work of carpenter ants, as these insects do not eat wood. They use it only as a building material. In this tree a colony of ants have gnawed out their many-chambered home.

Termites actually eat the wood they live in; there is never a mound of sawdust near their nests. This log was lying face down in the woods. On the underside, protected from light and air, a termite colony made these tunnels.

Termites avoid air and sunlight. They are blind and colorless, like most animals that live in the dark. The length of the wings on this termite indicates that it is almost fully grown. After the next molt, it may become an adult.

on the species. These cocoons are sold as "ant eggs" for fish and turtle food. (An actual ant egg is only one five-hundredth of an inch long—barely visible.) When an ant colony is disturbed, workers carry the pupae to safety in their jaws. This might seem a fine example of altruism but, in fact, the survival of the colony depends on the pupae being guarded.

Ant colonies seem to be organized much like human societies: some ants are hunters, some gather plant products like seeds or nectar, while others are agriculturalists, tending herds of aphid "cows" or raising fungi for food in their subterranean tunnels.

Hunter ants have well-developed stingers and kill the insects they find on their foraging trips. The soldier ants then take over, using their strong jaws to cut up the carcass—possibly a large caterpillar—into small pieces. The workers are then able to carry the bits home. The gatherers, and the farmers, have no stinger for attack, but can bite and squirt poison in self-defense.

Ants navigate in a variety of ways. Some follow scent trails which are made by a scout touching its abdomen to the ground periodically. Other ants, equipped with sensitive antennae, can easily follow its trail. Some ants have well-developed eyes and seem to locate landmarks visually. Still others seem to be able to navigate by using the sun as a compass. They are sensitive to the direction of the direct light rays from the sun.

Termites   Although they are frequently called "white ants," termites have nothing in common with ants except their colonial way of life. The two groups of insects are not even related, since ants, wasps, and bees comprise the order of Hymenoptera, while termites are more akin to cockroaches, and belong to the order Isoptera, meaning "equal wings." Termites are different in appearance, eat different food, and have a different social structure in the nest too.

Termites are broadbodied, lacking the slender waist of the ant. Nor do they have the navigating powers that ants have. They establish their nests close to, or sometimes in, a source of wood, and hardly ever emerge into the open. They avoid light and dry air, and if it is necessary to work above ground, they build covered tubes. Workers are blind and white, common features in animals that live in the dark.

Although both ants and termites may live in wood, there is one fundamental difference: to the carpenter ant, the wood is a building site—wood and sawdust must be removed to make galleries. But there is never any sawdust near a termite colony, for termites eat wood as well as live in it.

Wood is difficult to digest. Termites would starve to death if it were not for microscopic one-celled animals that live in their intestines. These protozoa produce chemicals that digest the wood so that it can be converted into energy by the termites. Because termites continually feed each other, the protozoa get a chance to infect all members of a colony. This symbiotic relationship, mutually beneficial to termites and protozoa, adds up to a hundred million dollars worth of wood damage every year in the United States.

Winged sexual forms, future kings and queens, are produced in the spring. These dark termites have two pairs of transparent wings longer than their bodies. The royal pair do not mate until after they have found a new nest site and shed their wings; after mating the king continues to live with the queen. She is more fortunate than the ant queen for her first batch of eggs develop to a useful stage more quickly. Instead of the ants' complete (four-stage) metamorphosis, termites have only three stages of change. The nymphs are able to work after their first of six molts. It has been said that a termite colony exploits child labor, whereas ant workers are adults.

In the termite colony, workers and soldiers can be either infertile males or females instead of exclusively female as in the ant system. There are reserve kings and queens, too, able to reproduce if something should happen to the reigning pair. The social structure is very complex, partly because the caste system is very flexible. Termites may even regress in caste, perhaps because of internal chemical changes, if there are not enough of a certain caste in the nest.

Only one species of termite lives in the eastern United States. It lives underground and subsists on dead wood. But in the tropics there are many species, some of which build cement-like nests that tower ten feet or more above the ground.

insect relatives

There are many different kinds of insects. However, insects as a group have many relatives, all of whom are similar to the insect in several respects: they all have jointed legs and also, they have a rigid exoskeleton, with growth occurring in spurts at the time of molting. Insects and their relatives belong to a large animal group called Arthropods, which means "jointed legs." Besides the insects, this group includes four other subgroups: arachnids (eight-leggers), crustaceans (ten-leggers), centipedes (hundred-leggers), and milli-pedes (thousand-leggers).

Eight-leggers   Spiders and mites, ticks and scorpions, as well as daddy longlegs have eight legs each, making it very easy to distinguish them from insects. Only spiders and scorpions are poisonous. Spiders have venom glands in their heads and hollow fangs to inject the poison; a scorpion's sting is at the end of the long curled abdomen.

Whether they are eight-eyed hunting spiders or almost blind web-spinners, spiders use their venom primarily to kill their food. The venom paralyzes the prey, which can be any small living creature of appropriate size. Then digestive fluids are poured on, and proteins in liquid form are absorbed. In spite of most housewives' instant reaction to spiders, they are actually very valuable, being a most effective control on insects. But unlike the more vora-cious eaters, spiders can live for as long as a year without food. (They do need water more often.)

Spiders' bodies have only two sections: the head and thorax form one unit, while the abdomen, with its complex arrangement of silk-producing spinnerets at the hind end, forms the other. Orb spiders spin geometrical traps to catch their food. They produce sticky silk for the spiral lines, and non-sticky silk— safe for them to walk along—for the spokes. Their egg cases, too, are made of silk. Hunting spiders spin no webs; they run after their food. They produce silk only to enclose a group of eggs in a cocoon.

Mites look much like extremely small spiders. A magnifying glass would be needed to count their eight legs. One bright red variety lives in ponds. Others are a nuisance to gardeners because they infest plants.

Ticks are extremely hard to kill because they are so flat and hard-bodied. Stepping on one is not likely to make it any flatter. They seem to be more numerous in the spring. They lurk on shrubs and plant stems with their legs outstretched, ready to hitchhike on any passerby, be he dog or man. Females need a meal of blood so that their eggs will mature, and once their mouthparts have taken hold of the skin of a warm-blooded animal, they are hard to remove. Touching them with alcohol or a very hot match seems to do the trick.

A string of segments makes up the millipede's body. Each segment has two pairs of short, jointed legs. When disturbed, it curls up into a tight coil.

The ten-legged sowbug breathes through gills, like its relative the lobster. But unlike the lobster, it lives on land. It is found in damp places under logs and stones.

Each segment of the centipede has only one pair of legs, but they are longer than the millipede's. A useful insect-eater, the centipede attacks its prey with fangs and poison.

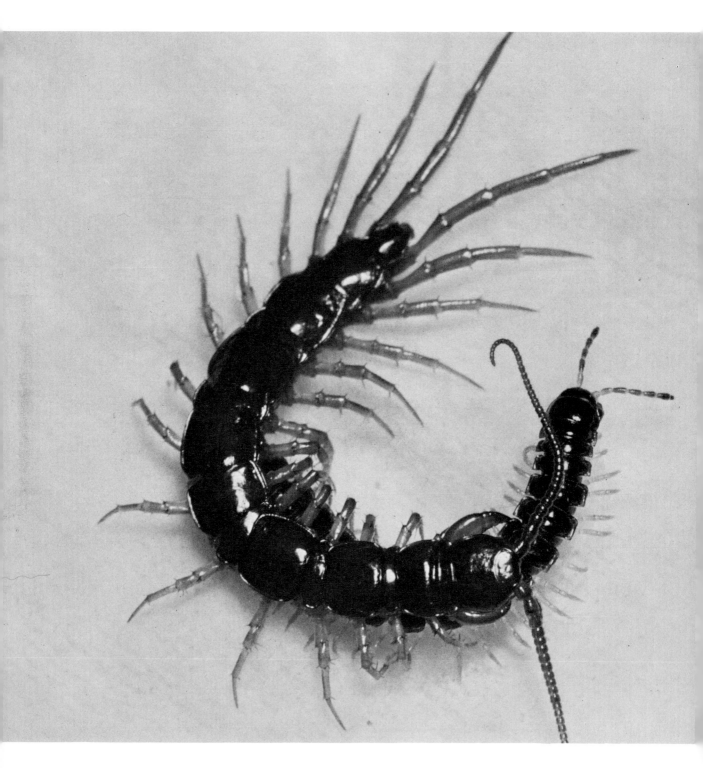

Under this fierce attack, the vegetarian millipede stands little chance of survival. The centipede will soon poison and eat its defenseless victim.

It's wise to check for ticks when returning from a walk in the country, for, in addition to their blood-thirstiness, they can also transmit diseases. And once they become established in a heated home they begin to reproduce at a fantastic rate (a female lays more than 5,000 eggs at once). Then it is even more difficult to exterminate them since ordinary insecticides are not effective.

Daddy longlegs represent no danger whatsoever to human beings in spite of the fear and dislike they seem to arouse. They do their hunting for insects on overcast days and at dusk, preferring to avoid the bright light. Also known as harvestmen, they have no stinging or biting equipment, nor are there antennae or silk glands. Eight long slender delicate legs support the seed-shaped body. Like crane flies, these long legs are not permanently attached, but can be released to avoid predators. The legs can be regrown at the next molt. Prowling in dense shrubbery or in dimly lit places, they do much to reduce the astronomical insect population.

Ten-leggers Crayfish, crabs, and lobsters, all crustaceans, are obvious ten-leggers. Their outside-skeletons are stiffened with deposits of lime extracted from water. Barnacles are not so obviously members of the group, but after a wandering youth, each barnacle settles down permanently on a rock or shell, builds a house of lime, stands on its head inside and then whenever the tide comes in, kicks food into its mouth with ten slender jointed legs.

Sowbugs, too, are crustaceans, the only ones that are able to live on land. Since they breathe by means of gills (as all crustaceans do), they are confined to damp places. If you turn over a log or rock in the woods, you will probably see a sowbug scurry for the dark, its armor-plated body shaped like a small flexible tank. They are sometimes called pillbugs because of their habit of curling up when disturbed, a position which protects the soft underparts.

Hundred-plus-leggers Millipedes and centipedes are called thousand- and hundred-leggers, but these are exaggerations. Millipedes may have a hundred pairs of jointed legs, but centipedes have only about two dozen pairs.

A millipede is made up of a cylindrical series of segments. On each segment there are two pairs of short jointed legs which move in waves as the creature progresses. Millipedes are vegetarians, and as such can be damaging to plants if they are numerous. When disturbed they curl into a tight coil.

Centipedes, on the other hand, are carnivorous. They have fangs and poison to kill their food, and their flattened bodies enable them to slither easily into crevices to hide. The combination of their long legs (one pair to each segment) and long antennae make them look dangerous. Housewives who find centipedes in sinks and tubs often promptly squash them (or get their husbands to), but centipedes really do more good than harm because of the many insects they eat.

135

Ordinarily, spiders hang their eggs in their webs. But the fisher spider spins no web, so the mother must carry the egg case around with her. After they hatch, the tiny spiderlings will ride on her back for a week or two. Then they will go off on their own.

The fisher spider has as many eyes as it has legs—eight in all. With no web to trap insects, this spider must hunt for them. These two rows of eyes help it find food.

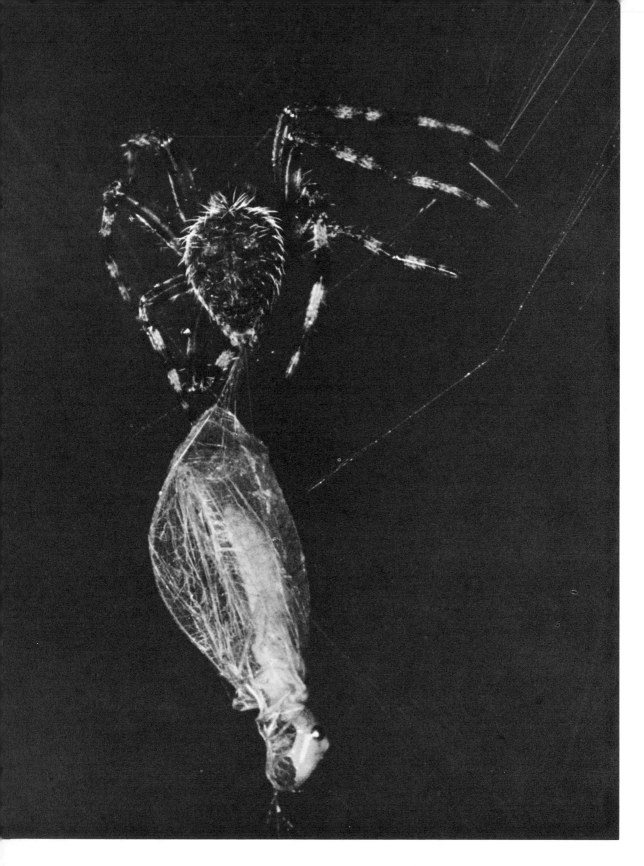

After trapping an insect in its loose web, this garden spider spins a firm silk wrapping around its victim. The lacewing inside is being saved for future meals.

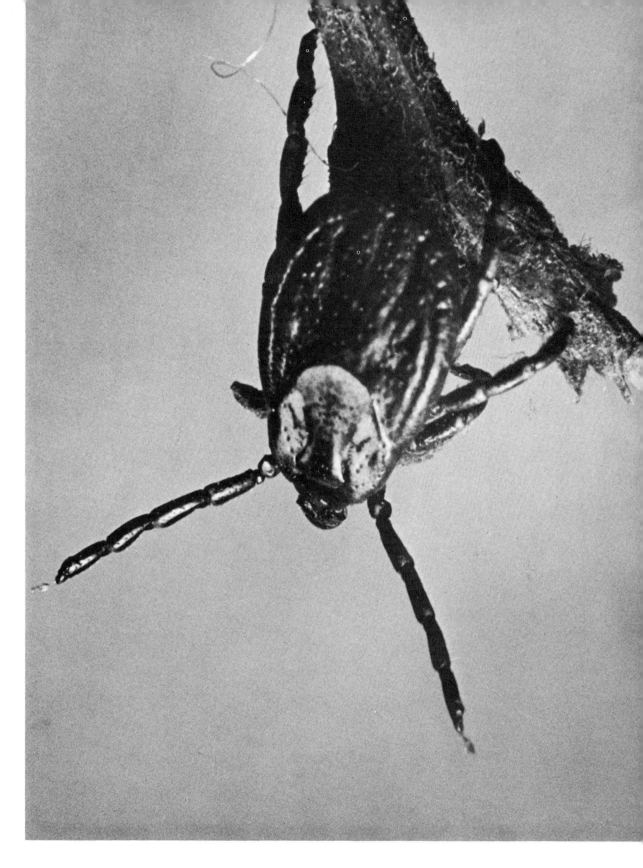

Ticks are hard to kill. Even stepping on them is not likely to crush their flat, hard bodies. In the spring they wait, arms outstretched, to hitch a ride on some warm-blooded animal. Then they sink their mouths into the animal's skin and suck its blood.

A daddy longlegs is supposed to have eight legs. But sometimes it sacrifices a leg to save its life. This lucky survivor has little to worry about — another leg will appear at its next molt.

A circular row of eyes provides the jumping spider with wide-angle vision. This tiny creature is found in the northeast. Unlike its desert relative, it has no stinger.

a note on
photographing insects

Taking pictures of insects isn't easy. They are an uncooperative, cantankerous group of animals, and provide a great challenge to any photographer. Here is a brief description of my encounters with the critters, and a few pointers that may help you photograph them too.

One of the best cameras for insect photography is the 35-mm single-lens reflex with interchangeable lenses, such as the Heiland Pentax H-3 or H-1 which I use. These cameras usually focus to within approximately eighteen inches, but one look through the viewfinder will quickly show you that this is not close enough for insects. To obtain greater magnification you must move the lens farther away from the film plane. This can be done with extension tubes or bellows. My choice is the bellows, for it gives much greater versatility in photographing a variety of subjects.

If you use the regular two-inch lens on the bellows you will get great magnification. However, since the lens is designed for focusing at two inches, better results will be obtained if the lens is reversed, for the lens is now much farther than two inches from the film plane. Personally, I prefer a lens with a longer focal length and a flat field. My favorite is an inexpensive Aetna Actinar 105-mm short-mount lens that I purchased from a mail order house for about $14 plus postage.

Either type of lens produces macrophotographs, that is, images larger than the actual object being photographed. This great magnification also magnifies the slightest camera movement, so that a solid tripod mount is essential to avoid blurred negatives. It also reduces depth of field severely when the diaphragm is wide open, as it usually must be for focusing. For actual shooting the lens should be stopped down as far as possible. Exposure is no problem with electronic flash. A modern unit gives ample illumination for small diaphragm settings, and the 1/500- to 1/2000-second flash effectively freezes most of the movement an insect might make when its picture is being taken.

When shooting in my basement studio, I use an old Braun Automatic flash unit that is nine years old, and still going strong. Although the manufacturer claims a rather high watt second output, I have found a Kodachrome II guide number of 56 produces properly exposed transparencies.

This rather large unit is fine at home, but when I take to the field I prefer the pocket size Mecablitz 110. While very small in size, it packs a terrific wallop in light output that gives a Kodachrome II guide number of 40.

Best results are obtained by closing the lens all the way down and controlling the exposure by varying the distance of the flash head from the subject. All sorts of magnification tables and exposure charts have been published, but it is best to tabulate your own chart. Standardize on one film-developer combination, and expose a series of negatives at various bellows extensions and electronic flash-head distances, carefully recording each exposure.

When I first began taking pictures of insects I ran the gamut of films from Tri X to KB-14 and developers from fine grain to vigorous. The combination that met all my requirements was Adox KB-14 developed in Rodinal. Excellent tonal range is achieved when the Rodinal is diluted 100 to 1, and the film developed for eighteen minutes at a 68° F. For a small tank, 3 cc. of Rodinal in 10 ounces of water, or for a large tank, 5 cc. in 16 2/3 ounces of water, gives the proper dilution.

Photographic technique is seldom a real problem. It's the insects that cause trouble. You can't use dead ones. If photographed dead, they really look dead. Legs assume all sorts of grotesque positions, antennae curl up, and wings go askew. The answer to all of this, of course, is to take their pictures when alive. But did you every try to get an angry hornet to sit still for its portrait?

For example, the little weevil on page 104 was an extremely uncooperative subject. After preparing the stage—a sixteen- by twenty-inch gray card behind a small branch stuck into a can of dirt, deciding on which leaf to place the subject, positioning my camera, focusing the lens, and placing the flash head at the proper distance from the point of focus, the little weevil refused to sit still for even five seconds. I used all the tricks I knew, including chilling in the refrigerator and dosing with carbon dioxide gas, but it seemed oblivious to anything designed to slow it down. It would either crawl under a leaf to get out of sight or scurry directly to the edge of the leaf and take off. I noticed, however, that when it reached the leaf edge, it would hesitate a few seconds, as if trying to decide which way to go before taking off. This was the clue I wanted, so I prefocused my camera on the edge of the leaf and got the picture I wanted.

I have tried many methods of subduing insects, but the two most successful are cold and carbon dioxide gas. Chilling is easiest, for you need only place the insect in a container and put it in the refrigerator for fifteen to thirty minutes. It will stay immobilized until it warms up. Don't place it in the freezer; this will stop it permanently.

The second, and best, method is anesthetizing with carbon dioxide gas.

This gas, used in making carbonated beverages and fire extinguishers, is quite common and easily available. However, the CO_2 containers designed for commercial use are inconvenient to use. They are too large and heavy, and they lack controllable valves for directing or metering the amount of gas you may wish to use. A small container of CO_2 gas with a controlling valve can be purchased from a medical supply house. A piece of plastic tubing attached to the exit valve gives more precise control of the gas. (You may need a doctor's prescription to buy a medical CO_2 cylinder; ask your family physician about this.)

One or two short bursts of CO_2 into a bottle or plastic container holding the insect will anesthetize it for from one to several minutes. This should give you ample time to pose your subject.

You will find the best insect pictures are taken under controlled conditions in your home or studio. Props, such as flowers, leaves, and dead twigs, and appropriate backgrounds all help to make better pictures and should be kept available for immediate use when needed.

Outside of patience, about the only other assistance you will need to photograph insects is a little knowledge of them. While some of their life histories are simple and others are quite complex, they seldom if ever vary in sequence. Armed with advance information secured from this and other books, you will be assured of fascinating pictures, as well as the reward of a deeper and better understanding of the fabulous world of insects.

HARRY F. BREVOORT

index